What the Twilight

WHAT THE TWILIGHT SAYS

Essays /

Derek Walcott

Farrar, Straus and Giroux

New York

Farrar, Straus and Giroux
19 Union Square West, New York 10003

Library of Congress Cataloging-in-Publication Data
Walcott, Derek.
    What the twilight says : essays / Derek Walcott. — 1st ed.
        p.   cm.
    ISBN 0-374-52683-4 (pbk.)
    I. Title.
PR9272.9.W3W48   1998
814—DC21   98-7391

The following essays originally appeared in these publications:
"What the Twilight Says": Dream on Monkey Mountain,
Farrar, Straus and Giroux, 1970; "The Muse of History": Is
Massa Day Dead?, ed. Orde Coombs (Anchor Books, 1974);
"The Antilles: Fragments of Epic Memory": Nobel Lecture,
December 7, 1992; "On Robert Lowell": The New York Review
of Books, March 1, 1984; "On Hemingway": Bostonia, May/
June 1990; "C.L.R. James": The New York Times Book
Review, March 25, 1984; "The Garden Path: V. S. Naipaul":
The New Republic, April 13, 1987; "Magic Industry: Joseph
Brodsky": The New York Review of Books, November 24,
1988; "The Master of the Ordinary: Philip Larkin": The New
York Review of Books, June 1, 1989; "Ted Hughes": London
Daily Telegraph, October 21, 1989; "Crocodile Dandy: Les
Murray": The New Republic, February 6, 1989; "The Road
Taken: Robert Frost": Homage to Robert Frost, Farrar, Straus
and Giroux, 1996; "A Letter to Chamoiseau": The New York
Review of Books, August 14, 1997; "Café Martinique: A Story":
House and Garden, 1985.

IN MEMORY J.B.

Contents

I

What the Twilight Says / 3

The Muse of History / 36

The Antilles: Fragments of Epic Memory / 65

II

On Robert Lowell / 87

On Hemingway / 107

C.L.R. James / 115

The Garden Path: V. S. Naipaul / 121

Magic Industry: Joseph Brodsky / 134

The Master of the Ordinary: Philip Larkin / 153

Ted Hughes / 176

Crocodile Dandy: Les Murray / 182

The Road Taken: Robert Frost / 193

A Letter to Chamoiseau / 213

III

Café Martinique: A Story / 235

I / 🌿

What the Twilight Says

I

But I see what it is, you are not from these parts, you don't know what our twilights can do. Shall I tell you?
—SAMUEL BECKETT, *Waiting for Godot*

When dusk heightens, like amber on a stage set, those ramshackle hoardings of wood and rusting iron which circle our cities, a theatrical sorrow rises with it, for the glare, like the aura from an old-fashioned brass lamp, is like a childhood signal to come home. Light in our cities keeps its pastoral rhythm, and the last home-going traffic seems to rush through darkness that comes from suburban swamp or forest in a noiseless rain. In true cities another life begins: neons stutter to their hysterical pitch, bars, restaurants, and cinemas blaze with artifice, and Mammon takes over the switchboard, manipulator of cities; but here the light makes our strongest buildings tremble, its colour hints of rust, more stain than air. To set out for rehearsals in that quivering quarter-hour is to engage conclusions, not beginnings, for one walks past the gilded hallucinations of poverty with a corrupt resignation touched by details, as if the destitute, in their orange-tinted back yards, under their dusty trees, or climbing to their favelas, were all natural scene designers and poverty were not a condition but an art. Deprivation is made lyrical, and twilight, with the patience of alchemy, almost transmutes despair into virtue. In the tropics nothing is lovelier than the allotments of the poor, no theatre is as vivid, voluble, and cheap.

Years ago, watching them, and suffering as you watched, you proffered silently the charity of a language which they could not speak, until your suffering, like the language, felt superior, estranged. The dusk was a raucous chaos of curses, gossip, and laughter; everything performed in public, but the voice of the inner language was reflective and mannered, as far above its subjects as that sun which would never set until its twilight became a metaphor for the withdrawal of empire and the beginning of our doubt.

Colonials, we began with this malarial enervation: that nothing could ever be built among these rotting shacks, barefooted back yards, and moulting shingles; that being poor, we already had the theatre of our lives. So the self-inflicted role of martyr came naturally, the melodramatic belief that one was message bearer for the millennium, that the inflamed ego was enacting their will. In that simple schizophrenic boyhood one could lead two lives: the interior life of poetry, the outward life of action and dialect. Yet the writers of my generation were natural assimilators. We knew the literature of empires, Greek, Roman, British, through their essential classics; and both the patois of the street and the language of the classroom hid the elation of discovery. If there was nothing, there was everything to be made. With this prodigious ambition one began.

If, twenty years later, that vision has not been built, so that at every dusk one ignites a city in the mind above the same sad fences where the poor revolve, the theatre still an architectural fantasy, if there is still nothing around us, darkness still preserves the awe of self-enactment as the sect gathers for its self-extinguishing, self-discovery rites. In that aboriginal darkness the first principles are still sacred, the grammar and movement of the body, the shock of the domesticated voice startling itself in a scream. Centuries of servitude have to be shucked; but there is no history, only the history of emotion. Pubescent ignorance comes into the light, a shy girl, eager to charm, and one's instinct is savage: to violate that ingenuousness, to degrade, to strip her of those values learnt from films and books because she too moves in her own hallucination: that of a fine and separate star, while her counterpart, the actor, sits watching, but he sits next to another hallucination, a doppelgänger released from his environment and his race. Their simplicity is really ambition. Their gaze is filmed with hope of departure. The noblest are those who are trapped, who have accepted the twilight.

If I see these as heroes it is because they have kept the sacred urge of actors everywhere: to record the anguish of the race. To do this, they must return through a darkness whose terminus is amnesia. The darkness which yawns before them is terrifying. It is the journey back from man to ape. Every actor should make this journey to articulate his origins, but for these who have been called not men but mimics, the darkness must be total, and the cave should not contain a single man-made, mnemonic object. Its noises should be elemental, the roar of rain, ocean, wind, and fire. Their first sound should be like the last, the cry. The voice must grovel in search of itself, until gesture and sound fuse and the blaze of their flesh astonishes them. The children of slaves must sear their memory with a torch. The actor must break up his body and feed it as ruminatively as ancestral storytellers fed twigs to the fire. Those who look from their darkness into the tribal fire must be bold enough to cross it.

The cult of nakedness in underground theatre, of tribal rock, of poverty, of rite, is not only nostalgia for innocence but the enactment of remorse for the genocides of civilization, a search for the wellspring of tragic joy in ritual, a confession of aboriginal calamity, for their wars, their concentration camps, their millions of displaced souls have degraded and shucked the body as food for the machines. These self-soiling, penitential cults, the Theatre of the Absurd, the Theatre of Cruelty, the Poor Theatre, the Holy Theatre, the pseudo-barbarous revivals of primitive tragedy are not threats to civilization but acts of absolution, gropings for the outline of pure tragedy, rituals of washing in the first darkness. Their howls and flagellations are cries to that lost God which they have pronounced dead, for the God who is offered to slaves must be served dead, or He may change His chosen people.

The colonial begins with this knowledge, but it has taken one twenty years to accept it. When one began twenty years ago it was in the faith that one was creating not merely a play but a theatre, and not merely a theatre but its environment. Then the twilight most resembled dawn, then how simple it all seemed! We would walk, like new Adams, in a nourishing ignorance which would name plants and people with a child's belief that the world is its own age. We had no more than children need, and perhaps we have remained childish, because fragments of that promise still surprise us. Then, even the old rules were exciting! Imitation was pure belief. We, the actors and poets, would strut like new Adams in a nakedness where sets, costumes, dimmers, all the "dirty devices" of the theatre were unnecessary or inaccessible. Poverty seemed a gift to the imagination, necessity was truly a virtue, so we set our plays in the open, in natural, unphased light, and our subject was bare, "unaccommodated man." Today one writes this with more exhaustion than pride, for that innocence has been corrupted and society has taken the old direction. In these new nations art is a luxury and the theatre the most superfluous of amenities.

Every state sees its image in those forms which have the mass appeal of sport, seasonal and amateurish. Stamped on that image is the old colonial grimace of the laughing nigger, steelbandsman, carnival masker, calypsonian, and limbo dancer. These popular artists are trapped in the state's concept of the folk form, for they preserve the colonial demeanour and threaten nothing. The folk arts have become the symbol of a carefree, accommodating culture, an adjunct to tourism, since the state is impatient with anything which it cannot trade.

This is not what a generation envisaged twenty years ago, when a handful of childish visionaries foresaw a republic devoted to the industry of art, for in those days we had nothing else. The theatre was about us, in the streets, at lampfall in the kitchen doorway, but nothing was solemnised into cultural significance. We recognized illiteracy for what it was, a defect, not the attribute it is now considered to be by revolutionaries. Language was earned, there was no self-contempt, no vision of revenge. Thus, for the young poet and actor, there was no other motivation but knowledge. The folk knew their deprivations and there were no frauds to sanctify them. If the old gods were dying in the mouths of the old, they died of their own volition. Today they are artificially resurrected by the anthropologist's tape recorder and in the folk archives of departments of culture.

To believe in its folk forms the state would have to not only hallow its mythology but rebelieve in dead gods, not as converts either, but as makers. But no one in the New World whose one God is advertised as dead can believe in innumerable gods of another life. Those gods would have to be an anthropomorphic variety of his will.

Our poets and actors would have not only to describe possession but to enact it, otherwise we would have not art but blasphemy, and blasphemy which has no fear is decoration. So now we are entering the "African" phase with our pathetic African carvings, poems, and costumes, and our art objects are not sacred vessels placed on altars but goods placed on shelves for the tourist. The romantic darkness which they celebrate is thus another treachery, this time perpetrated by the intellectual. The result is not one's own thing but another minstrel show. When we produced Soyinka's masterpiece *The Road*, one truth, like the murderous headlamps of his mammy-wagons, transfixed us, and this was that our frenzy goes by another name, that it is this naming, ironically enough, which weakens our effort at being African. We tried, in the words of his professor, to "hold the god captive," but for us, Afro-Christians, the naming of the god estranged him. Ogun was an exotic for us, not a force. We could pretend to enter his power, but he would never possess us, for our invocations were not prayer but devices. The actor's approach could not be catatonic but rational; expository, not receptive. However, Ogun is not a contemplative but a vengeful force, a power to be purely obeyed. Like the professor, only worse, we had lost both gods, and only blasphemy was left.

Since art is informed by something beyond its power, all we could successfully enact was a dance of doubt. The African revival is escape to another dignity, but one understands the glamour of its simplifications. Listen, one kind of writer, generally the entertainer, says, "I will write in the language of the people however gross or incomprehensible"; another says: "Nobody else go' understand this, you hear, so le' me write English"; while the third is dedicated to purifying the language of the tribe, and it is he who is jumped on by both sides for pretentiousness or playing white. He is the mulatto of style. The traitor. The assimilator. Yes. But one did not say to his Muse, "What kind of language is this that you've given me?" as no liberator asks history, "What kind of people is that that I'm meant to ennoble?," but one went about his father's business. Both fathers'. If the language was contemptible, so were the people. After one had survived the adolescence of prejudice there was nothing to justify. Once the New World black had tried to prove that he was as good as his master, when he should have proven not his equality but his difference. It was this distance that could command attention without pleading for respect. My generation had looked at life with black skins and blue eyes, but only our own painful, strenuous looking, the learning of looking, could find meaning in the life around us, only our own strenuous hearing, the hearing of our hearing, could make sense of the sounds we made. And without comparisons. Without any startling access of "self-respect." Yet most of our literature loitered in the pathos of sociology, self-pitying and patronized. Our writers whined in the voices of twilight, "Look at this people! They may be degraded, but they are as good as you are. Look at what you have done to them." And their poems remained laments, their novels propaganda tracts, as if one general apology on behalf of the past would supplant imagination, would spare them the necessity of great art. Pastoralists of the African revival should know that what is needed is not new names for old things, or old names for old things, but the faith of using the old names anew, so that mongrel as I am, something prickles in me when I see the word "Ashanti" as with the word "Warwickshire," both separately intimating my grandfathers' roots, both baptizing this neither proud nor ashamed bastard, this hybrid, this West Indian. The power of the dew still shakes off of our dialects, which is what Césaire sings:

Storm, I would say. River, I would command. Hurricane, I would say. I would utter "leaf." Tree. I would be drenched in all the rains, soaked in all the dews.

I I

Et c'est l'heure, O Poète, de décliner ton nom, ta naissance, et ta race . . .
—ST.-JOHN PERSE, *Exil*

Yes. But we were all strangers here. The claim which we put forward now as Africans is not our inheritance but a bequest, like that of other races, a bill for the condition of our arrival as slaves. Our own ancestors shared that complicity, and there is no one left on whom we can exact revenge. That is the laceration of our shame. Nor is the land automatically ours because we were made to work it. We have no more proprietorship as a race than have the indentured workers from Asia except the claim is wholly made. By all the races as one race, because the soil was stranger under our own feet than under those of our captors. Before us they knew the names of the forests and the changes of the sea, and theirs were the names we used. We began again, with the vigour of a curiosity that gave the old names life, that charged an old language, from the depth of suffering, with awe. To the writers of my generation, then, the word, and the ritual of the word in print, contained this awe, but the rage for revenge is hard to exorcise.

At nineteen, an elate, exuberant poet madly in love with English, but in the dialect-loud dusk of water buckets and fish sellers, conscious of the naked, voluble poverty around me, I felt a fear of that darkness which had swallowed up all fathers. Full of precocious rage, I was drawn, like a child's mind to fire, to the Manichean conflicts of Haiti's history. The parallels were there in my own island, but not the heroes: a black French island somnolent in its Catholicism and black magic, blind faith and blinder overbreeding, a society which triangulated itself medievally into land baron, serf, and cleric, with a vapid, highbrown bourgeoisie. The fire's shadows, magnified into myth, were those of the black Jacobins of Haiti.

They were Jacobean, too, because they flared from a mind drenched in Elizabethan literature out of the same darkness as Webster's Flamineo, from a flickering world of mutilation and heresy. They were moved by the muse of witchcraft, their self-disgust foreshadowed ours, that wrestling contradiction of being white in mind and black in body, as if the flesh were coal from which the spirit like tormented smoke writhed to escape. I repeat the raging metaphysics of a bewildered boy in this rhetoric. I can relive, without his understanding, a passion which I have betrayed. But they seemed to him, then, those slave-kings, Dessalines and Christophe, men who had structured their own despair. Their tragic bulk was massive as a citadel at twilight. They were our only noble ruins. He believed then that the moral of tragedy could only be Christian, that their fate was the debt exacted by the sin of pride, that they were punished by a white God as masters punished servants for presumption. He saw history as hierarchy, and to him these heroes, despite their meteoric passages, were damned to the old darkness because they had challenged an ordered universe. He was in awe of their blasphemy, he rounded off their fate with the proper penitence, while during this discipleship which he served as devotedly as any embittered acolyte, the young Frantz Fanon and the already ripe and bitter Césaire were manufacturing the homemade bombs of their prose poems, their drafts for revolution, in the French-creole island of Martinique. They were blacker. They were poorer. Their anguish was tragic and I began to feel deprived of blackness and poverty. I had my own divisions, too, but it was only later, when their prophecies became politics, that I was confronted with choice. My bitterness matched theirs, but it concealed envy; my compassion was not less, but both were full of self-contempt and contained a yearning. Those first heroes of the Haitian revolution, to me, their tragedy lay in their blackness. Yet one had more passion then, passion for reconciliation as well as change. It is no use repeating that this was not the way the world went, that the acolyte would have to defrock himself of that servitude. Now one may see such heroes as squalid fascists who chained their own people, but they had size, mania, the fire of great heretics.

It is easy, twenty years later, to mock such ambition, to concede what a critic called its "fustian," yet the Jacobean style, its cynical, aristocratic flourish, came naturally to this first play—the corruption of slaves into tyrants. Here were slaves who by divine right could never be kings, because by claiming kingship they abrogated the law of God. Despite my race, I could not believe that He would choose such people as His engines. Still, this tragedy's fiercest exchanges contained a self-frightening fury:

ARCHBISHOP
This is the curse of the nation,
Eating your own stomach, where the sickness is,
Your smell of blood offends the nostrils of God.

CHRISTOPHE
Perhaps the smell of sweat under my arms
offends that god too, quivering his white, crooked nostrils;
Well, tell him, after death, that it is honest
as the seven words of blood broken on his flesh, tell Him
the nigger smell that even kings must wear
is bread and wine to life.
I am proud, I have worked and grown
This country to its stature, tell Him that.

The theme has remained: one race's quarrel with another's God.

There was only one noble ruin in the archipelago: Christophe's massive citadel at La Ferrière. It was a monument to egomania, more than a strategic castle; an effort to reach God's height. It was the summit of the slave's emergence from bondage. Even if the slave had surrendered one Egyptian darkness for another, that darkness was his will, that structure an image of the inaccessible achieved. To put it plainer, it was something we could look up to. It was all we had.

III

I am thinking of a child's vow sworn in vain,
Never to leave that valley his fathers called their home.
—YEATS

To be born on a small island, a colonial backwater, meant a precocious resignation to fate. The shoddy, gimcrack architecture of its one town, its doll-sized verandahs, jalousies and lacy eaves neatly perforated as those doilies which adorn the polished tables of the poor seemed so frail that the only credible life was nature. A nature without man, like the sea on which the sail of a canoe can seem an interruption. A nature with blistered aspects: grey, rotting shacks, the colour of the peasant woman's dress, which huddled on rocky rises outside the villages. But through nature one came to love the absence of philosophy, and fatally, perhaps, the beauty of certain degradations.

In that innocent vagabondage one sought out the poor as an adventure, an illumination, only to arrive where, rooted like a rigid articulation of the rocks, the green-and-blue-enamelled statue of the Virgin leaned from her niche, facing a green-and-blue Atlantic, like the peeling figurehead of a slave ship (in her various shrines her

age could change from decorous matron to eager postu-
lant), and where, back in the bleached, unpainted fishing
village streets everyone seemed salted with a reek of despair, a life, a theatre, reduced to elementals. The acrid,
shuttered smell of the poor was as potent and nocturnal
as the odours of sex, with its intimacies of lowered Virgin
lamps and coconut-fibre mattresses, until it seemed that
a Catholic destitution was a state of grace which being
part-white and Methodist I could never achieve. That life
was measured as carefully as broken shop bread by its rituals, it had dimpled the serene smile of Our Lady of the
Rocks by its observance of five o'clock Mass, rosaries,
scapulars, coloured prints, lampions with perpetual flame
floating in oil, vespers, fasts, feasts, and the shell-bordered
cemeteries by the village river. The race was locked in its
conviction of salvation like a freemasonry. There was more
envy than hate towards it, and the love that stubbornly
emerged showed like weeds through the ruined aisle of an
abandoned church, and one worked hard for that love,
against their love of priest and statue, against the pride of
their resignation. One worked to have the "feel" of the
island, bow, gunwales, and stern as jealously as the fisherman knew his boat, and, despite the intimacy of its size,
to be as free as a canoe out on the ocean.

That apprenticeship would mean nothing unless life
were made so real that it stank, so close that you could
catch the changes of morning and afternoon light on the
rocks of the Three Sisters, pale brown rocks carious in the
gargle of sea, could catch the flash of a banana leaf in
sunlight, catch the smell of drizzled asphalt and the always
surprisingly stale smell of the sea, the reek that chafes in
the guts of canoes, and the reek of human rags that you
once thought colorful, but, God give you that, in rage, a
reek both fresh and resinous, all salted on the page, that
dark catalogue of country-shop smells, the tang of raw,
fine powdery cod, of old onions drying, of the pork barrel,

and the shelves of faded cloth, all folded round the fusty smell of the proprietor, some exact magical, frightening woman in tinted glasses, who emerged from the darkness like history.

There the materials began. They were given.

And the fishermen, those whom Jesus first drew to His net, they were the most blasphemous and bitter.

Theirs was a naked, pessimistic life, crusted with the dirty spume of beaches. They were a sect which had evolved its own signs, a vocation which excluded the stranger. The separation of town from countryside and countryside from sea challenged your safety, and all one's yearning was to enter that life without living it. It smelled strong and true. But what was its truth?

That in the "New Aegean" the race, of which these fishermen were the stoics, had grown a fatal adaptability. As black absorbs without reflection they had rooted themselves with a voracious, unreflecting calm. By all arguments they should have felt displaced, seeing this ocean as another Canaan, but that image was the hallucination of professional romantics, writer and politician. Instead, the New World Negro was disappointingly ordinary. He needed to be stirred into bitterness, thence perhaps to action, which means that he was as avaricious and as banal as those who had enslaved him. What would deliver him from servitude was the forging of a language that went beyond mimicry, a dialect which had the force of revelation as it invented names for things, one which finally settled on its own mode of inflection, and which began to create an oral culture of chants, jokes, folksongs, and fables; this, not merely the debt of history, was his proper claim to the New World. For him metaphor was not a symbol but conversation, and because every poet begins with such ignorance, in the anguish that every noun will be freshly, resonantly named, because a new melodic inflection meant a new mode, there was no better beginning.

It did not matter how rhetorical, how dramatically heightened the language was if its tone was true, whether its subject was the rise and fall of a Haitian king or a small-island fisherman, and the only way to re-create this language was to share in the torture of its articulation. This did not mean the jettisoning of "culture" but, by the writer's making creative use of his schizophrenia, an electric fusion of the old and the new.

So the people, like the actors, awaited a language. They confronted a variety of styles and masks, but because they were casual about commitment, ashamed of their speech, they were moved only by the tragicomic and farcical. The tragicomic was another form of self-contempt. They considered tragedy to be, like English, an attribute beyond them.

IV

Clouds of heroes, young and old have died for me.
—JEAN GENET'S QUEEN IN *The Blacks*

The future of West Indian militancy lies in art. All revolutions begin amateurishly, with forged or stolen weapons, but the West Indian artist knew the need for revolt without knowing what weapons to use, and just as a comfortable, self-hugging pathos hid in the most polemical of West Indian novels, so there was in the sullen ambition of the West Indian actor a fear that he lacked proper weapons, that his voice, colour, and body were no match for the civilized concepts of theatre. This is an endemic evil that cannot be dissolved by professional hatred or by bitter flaunting of his race. In his encounter with a tawdry history he was shaken by judgements of this sort:

There has been romance, but it has been the romance of pirates and outlaws. The natural graces of life do not show themselves under such conditions. There has been no saint in the West Indies since Las Casas, no hero unless philo-Negro enthusiasm can make one out of Toussaint. There are no people there in the true sense of the word, with a character and purpose of their own.

This is the tone used of canaille, but it is canaille who, in exasperation at this truth, begin revolutions.

The pride of the colonial in the culture of his mother country was fiercer than her true children's, because the colonial feared to lose her. The most conservative and prejudiced redoubts of imperialism are in those who have acquired that patina through strenuous reverence: her judges and, ironically enough, her artists. My generation since its colonial childhood had no true pride but awe. We had not yet provided ourselves with heroes, and when the older heroes went out of fashion, or were stripped, few of us had any choice but to withdraw into a cave where we could scorn those who struggled in the heat. Change was too subterranean for us to notice. Our melodramatic instincts demanded sudden upheavals, and found nothing in the Roman patience of legal reforms. We became infuriated at the banal demands of labourer and peasant. We romanticized the poor. But the last thing which the poor needed was the idealization of their poverty. No play could be paced to the repetitive, untheatrical patience of hunger and unemployment. Hunger produces enervation of will and knows one necessity. Although in very few of the islands are people reduced to such a state, the empire of hunger includes work that is aimed only at necessities. It's inevitable that any playwright, knowing that this is his possible audience, will be concerned with deprivation as his major theme. So the sparse body of West Indian theatre still feeds on the subject of emaciation and what it produces: rogues, drunkards, madmen, outcasts, and sets against this the pastoral of the peasant. Its comedy begins with the premise that all are starved or deprived, or defend themselves from being further deprived by threats. Hunger induces its delirium, and it is this fever for heroic examples that can produce the glorification of revenge.

Yet revenge is a kind of vision. The West Indian mind historically hungover, exhausted, prefers to take its revenge in nostalgia, to narrow its eyelids in a schizophrenic daydream of an Eden that existed before its exile. Its fixation is for the breasts of a nourishing mother, and this is true not only of the generations of slaves' children but of those brought here through indigence or necessity, in fact, through the threat of hunger. But the communities maintain a half-brother relationship threatened by jealousies and suspicion. There is more romance in anthropology than there is in ordinary life, and our quarrels about genealogy, our visionary plays about the noble savage remain provincial, psychic justifications, strenuous attempts to create identity; yet there is nothing atavistic about our desires except that easy nostalgia which John Hearne has described. Once we have lost our wish to be white, we develop a longing to become black, and those two may be different, but are still careers. "The status of native is a nervous condition introduced and maintained by the settler among colonised people *with their consent*," says Sartre, introducing Fanon, and the new black continues that condition. His crimes are familial, litigious, his hatred is turned inward. The law is all he can remember of his past. Slaves, the children of slaves, colonials, then pathetic, unpunctual nationalists, what have we to celebrate? First, we have not wholly sunk into our own landscapes, as one gets the feeling at funerals that our bodies make only light, unlasting impressions on our earth. It is not an earth that has been fed long with the mulch of cultures, with the cycles of tribalism, feudalism, monarchy, democracy, industrialization. Death, which fastens us to the earth, remains pastoral or brutish, because no single corpse contributes to some tiered concept of a past. Everything is immediate, and this immediacy means overbreeding, illegitimacy, migration without remorse. The sprout casually stuck in the soil. The depth of being rooted is related to the shallowness of racial despair. The migratory West Indian feels rootless on his own earth, chafing at its beaches.

V

Whosoever will, whosoever will . . .
Hear the loving Father
Call the wanderer home
Whosoever will may come . . .
—Salvation Army hymn

A gas lamp startles the sidewalk and catches like fire-edged coals the black faces of men in white, martial uniforms, dilating the dun goatskin of the big bass drum, throwing its tireless radiance as far as our balcony across the street, changing the crossroads of Mary Ann Street and the Chaussée to a stage crossed by shadows. The recruiting patrol was Protestant, and their beat, thudding so loud that the stars shook, was to drum an army of Catholics into service by the joy of their performance, to arrest whoever paused, to draw children in a ring around the lantern light until there would be more than spectators: an unheard army singing in the pebbled back yards, in the jalousied upstairs bedrooms whose moonlit linen would have to wait. And if there was, too rarely, a brass cornet played by some silver-headed English adjutant, its high note striking sparks from the tin roofs, then a kind of marching would begin, but one that kept the native beat. Yet, like the long, applauded note, joy soared farther from two pale children staring from their upstairs window, wanting to march with that ragged, barefooted crowd, but who could not because they were not black and poor, until for one

of them, watching the shouting, limber congregation, that
difference became a sadness, that sadness rage, and that
longing to share their lives ambition, so that at least one
convert was made. They were the shadows of his first theatre, just as, at Christmas in the streets the Devil in red
underwear, with a hemp beard, a pitchfork, and a mon-
strously packed crotch, backed by a molasses-smeared
chorus of imps, would perform an elaborate Black Mass
of resurrection at the street corners. He and his brother
were already creating their own little theatre, "little men"
made from twigs enacting melodramas of hunting and escape, but of cowboys and gangsters, not of overseers and
maroons. On the verandah, with his back to the street, he
began marathon poems on Greek heroes which ran out of
breath, lute songs, heroic tragedies, but these rhythms, the
Salvation Army parodies, the Devil's Christmas songs, and
the rhythms of the street itself were entering the pulse
beat of the wrist.

I do not remember if they played at savages with their
cheap puppets; certainly poverty was never dramatized,
but what must have come out of all this later was a guilt;
a guilt as well as an envy. One could envy the poor then,
their theatre where everything was possible, sex, obscenity,
absolution, freedom, and not only the freedom to wander
barefoot but the freedom made from necessity, the freedom to hack down forests, to hollow canoes, to hunt
snakes, to fish, and to develop bodies made of tarred rope
that flung off beads of sweat like tightened fish lines.
There were other theatres, too. There was the theatre of
degeneracy. Not clouds of heroes but of flies. The derelicts
who mimed their tragedies, the lunatics who every day
improvised absurd monodramas, blasphemous, scabrous
monologues, satirists, cripples, alcoholics, one transves-
tite, one reprieved murderer, several hunched, ant-crazy
old women, including one who paused in the middle of
the street to address her feet and reprimand the sun, one

other fantasist dressed in black silk hat, gloves, frock coat, soiled spats and cane, another, a leg lost, bucking like a sailor, one parched, ravaged poet, ex-athlete and piano fiend; all towns are full of them, but their determined, self-destructive desolation was performed. Johnnie Walker, Pepsi-Cola, Wild Bill Hickok, Cat Strangler, Fowl Thief, Baz the Dead, Wax-me-all-over-except-my-balls, Bull-voiced Deighton, Submarine the Bum-Boatman, the untranslatable N'Homme Mama Migrains (your louse's mother's man), Lestrade sallow and humped like a provincial Sherlock Holmes, Estefine Manger Farine, and the inestimable Greene, Bap, Joumard, and Vorn.

And there were vampires, witches, gardeurs, masseurs (usually a fat black foreign-smelling blackness, with gold-rimmed spectacles), not to mention the country where the night withheld a whole, unstarred mythology of flaming, shed skins. Best of all, in the lamplit doorway at the creaking hour, the stories sung by old Sidone, a strange croaking of Christian and African songs. The songs, mainly about lost children, were sung in a terrible whine. They sang of children lost in the middle of a forest, where the leaves' ears pricked at the rustling of devils, and one did not know whether to weep for the first two brothers of every legend, one strong, the other foolish. All these sank like a stain. And taught us symmetry. The true folktale concealed a structure as universal as the skeleton, the one armature from Br'er Anancy to King Lear. It kept the same digital rhythm of three movements, three acts, three moral revelations, whether it was the tale of three sons or of three bears, whether it ended in tragedy or happily ever after. It had sprung from hearthside or lamplit hut door in an age when the night outside was a force, inimical, infested with devils, wood demons, a country for the journey of the soul, and any child who has heard its symmetry chanted would want to retell it when he was his own storyteller, with the same respect for its shape. The apparent conservatism of West Indian fiction, whether in fiction or in theatre, is not an imitative respect for moulds but a memory of that form.

Years later in another island you have formed a company so intimate that they have become limbs, extensions of your sensibility. You are rehearsing *The Blacks*, and you begin to see that their minds, whatever the variety of their education, are baffled by this challenge of the absurd. They resist the emphatic gaiety of that dance at the edge of the abyss. Its despair is another mimicry. They have the confused vitality of beginners, and like all beginners they are humanists. Presented with Genet's black and white dumb show, its first half a negative, its second half a print, the actors hesitate to recognize their images.

It may have to do with those subterranean charges that explode in their faces, for the play is mined with blinding flashes that cause a painful laughter. They catch, sidewise in the mirror of another's face, images of what they have feared, projections of their own caricatures. But their genius is not violent, it is comic. The play becomes less a satire and more a Carnival. Their joy is its root. The madness of surrealism means nothing to their sensibility, and this lack is not a question of culture but simply that their minds refuse to be disfigured. An actor feels a play through the nerves, not through the brain, and his instinct is to feel his body move, to tingle towards gesture, towards promiscuous exchange with fellow actors. It is not that they do not understand the absurd, but that they cannot enjoy its mincing, catamite dances of death. But as their society avoids truths, as their Carnival is a noise that fears everything, too many of the actors avoid the anguish of self-creation. So one closes West Indian plays in despair. Closes, and reopens them in the hope that the last, twilight-sodden sigh is mistaken and that morning will vigorously bring a stronger, exhilarating despair; not a despair that belongs to others but a truly tragic joy. It is our damnation to sigh not only for the amenities of civilization, its books, its women, its theatres, but also for its philosophies; and when revenge is the mode and a black angst fashionable, or when deprivation is made a cult-guilt of our artists, we find ourselves enraged. We imitate the images of ourselves.

An actor rises to a text and his tongue stumbles on words that have less immediacy than his dialect, and he collapses, or fakes difficulty, abashed. He confronts proper speech as his body once confronted certain "inflexible" classic gestures. He stands torn by the wish to amuse or to illuminate his people.

For imagination and body to move with original instinct, we must begin again from the bush. That return journey, with all its horror of rediscovery, means the annihilation of what is known. Some of our poets have pretended that journey, but with an itinerary whose resting points are predetermined. On such journeys the mind will discover what it chooses, and what these writers seek, like refugees raking debris, are heirlooms to dignify an old destitution. Even this destitution, carefully invoked, is pastoral. But if the body could be reduced once more to learning, to a rendering of things through groping mnemonic fingers, a new theatre could be made, with a delight that comes in roundly naming its object. Out of it, with patience, new reverberations would come. Yet this, too, the haemophilic twilight said, with its sapping of the will before rehearsals: "Bourgeois, safe in a vague, pastoral longing, you pretend to re-enter the bush, to imitate the frenzy of ancestral possession, your soul, with a fetid dampness, drifts between two temples, and the track to the grove is fenced." You despise the banal vigour of a future, where the folk art, the language, the music, like the economy, will accommodate itself to the centre of power, which is foreign, where people will simplify themselves to be clear, to be immediately apprehensible to the transient. The lean, sinewy strength of the folk dance has been fattened and sucked into the limbo of the nightclub, the hotel cabaret, and all the other prostitutions of a tourist culture: before you is the vision of a hundred Havanas and mini-Miamis, and who dares tell their Tourism Boards and Cultural Development Committees that the blacks in bondage at least had the resilience of their dignity, a knowledge of their degradation, while their descendants have gone both flaccid and colourful, covering their suffering with artificial rage or commercial elation? Even the last one among us who knows the melodies of the old songs fakes his African, becoming every season, by Kodak exposure of his cult, a phony shaman, a degraded priest. The urge towards the metropolitan language was the same as political deference to its centre, but the danger lay in confusing, even imitating the problems of the metropolis by pretensions to its power, its styles, its art, its ideas, and its concept of what we are. The core of this conflict was whether only a true city, by which one meant the metropolitan power, could nourish a theatre, or whether our cities, lacking all power, could be called cities at all. Ironically enough, the theatre at the heart of the metropolis was trying to reduce power to tribal simplicities of penitence and celebration, while our politics, as well as our arts, strove for sophistry, even to the point of imitated decadence. For our frustrated avant-gardists and our radicals there was neither enough power nor enough decadence to justify experiment; they missed our Sade, our Grotowski or the madness of an Artaud. While others, reactionaries in dashikis, screamed for the pastoral vision, for a return to nature over the loudspeaker. It was always the fate of the West Indian to meet himself coming back, and he would discover the power of simplicity, the graces of his open society, only after others had embraced it as a style.

VI

> *Hence our confirmed lack of culture is astonished by certain gran-*
> *diose anomalies; for example, on an island without any contact with*
> *modern civilization, the mere passage of a ship carrying only healthy*
> *passengers may provoke the sudden outbreak of diseases unknown*
> *on that island but a specialty of nations like our own: shingles,*
> *influenza, grippe, rheumatism, sinusitis, polyneuritis, etc.*
> —ANTONIN ARTAUD, *The Theatre and Its Double*

I try to divert my concentration from that mesmeric gritted oyster of sputum on the concrete floor of a tin-roofed shed in back of a choirmaster's house, half shango chapel, half Presbyterian country vestry, but there are two people circling that filthy asterisk in search of a gramophone needle which the choirmaster bewails that he bought just, just this morning, with our bewilderment before the screw-ups of technology, as if the gramophone vindictively insisted that their voices should be enough and had magisterially withdrawn its contribution. The women of the choir are dressed in the standard imitation frippery of Mexican or Venezuelan peasants: black skirts appliquéd with cushion-sized flowers, low-necked, lace-edged cotton bodices, and prim shoes, the plainest of the women with, unless argument is dominating memory, a lurid bloody hibiscus in her greased hair. The men are modestly dressed. Onstage, they might wear the three-quarter-length cotton trousers of the peon, and, if they were dancers, rainbow-rippled sleeves, more feminine than androgynous. Piquancy, charm have already emasculated those. Their dances have been refined to a female essence, a grinning fragility, suffocating as cheap perfume, their jetés and turns false as the coquetry of the women whose sex at least pullulates with the appeal of sweating crotches, while the men, the finer-boned the better, can offer nothing but their tightened, scrotum-packed costumes and witty backsides. Leave that alone.

It's whoredom and they will be paid. We are gathered here for something votive, and the choir men have a Protestant demureness, an inward smiling modesty.

But the night degenerates from decency to decency, offering, as though they were the shredded flesh and tree-sapped blood of the Saviour, the little cakes, sweets, thinned drinks and papery crisps of processed corn, plantain, potato, even the last vegetal gods dried and distributed. Then they begin to sing. They sing from what they have learnt from movies. They have acquired presentation, style. This consists of the women swaying gently from side to side without quite holding the edges of their flared skirts, like a child reciting, swaying their pressed heads, rounding their mouths, flirting with their eyes, and bowing, Jesus! bowing neatly, with the practiced modesty of professionals, except that the bow does not quite work like the professional's wry, screw-you-if-you-didn't-like-it smile; no, it contains the shrunken pride of the Community Centre, the ambition of social achievement. The sour constipated earth is hard as cement. Once their heels, like the heels of the drummer's palms on the carcass of the drum, would have made it resound. The worst song, the most sincerely sung, is an original, an anthem to the nation. The sentiments are infantile (though children are innocent of patriotism), the words and phrasing execrable. But the passion with which it is sung is its most desolating aspect. Furiously ungrammatical, emphatically crude, but patinaed with grace. It smells as soon as it is aired. It sickens everything, as crude and as natural as that dusted globule of splayed spit that has become the itch of your whole body. The flashing banana leaves, the thick, hot air, the thick, black voices straining for refinement, all these are mixed in one hallucination, slowly stunning into acceptance, if one is not to feel the old madness creaking the skull open again; the jet of spit on the gritty cement floor repeats, converts itself into saying, Well, it is all very touching and simple, it is sincere, it is real. Those dusty banana fronds are real, the gold teeth, and their thin gold watches, and the careful articulation of their small talk; and it is only you who are unnecessary, unreal. To create your reality, you must become part of them, spit, applaud, touch, eat with and sing with them, but what really sings in the dark hole of the heart is hollowness, what screams is something lost, something so embarrassed, like an animal that abandons its dying image in its cub, and moves deeper into bush. They are glad to see it go. I can feel it gone. It is gone in the precise signalling of those fine, fixed stars. Gone, with an odour of choking talc and perfume. Later, after the smiling minister goes, and the distinguished guests, of which you are one, the drumming and the true singing jerked alive by the rum and the furiously sweating night, all that straining after the old truth may begin, but the bored animal has gone to sleep. It is too late. Too late.

VII

The only escape was drama.
—V. S. NAIPAUL

All these are affirmations of identity, however forced. Our bodies think in one language and move in another, yet it should have become clear, even to our newest hybrid, the black critic who accuses poets of betraying dialect, that the language of exegesis is English, that the manic absurdity would be to give up thought because it is white. In our self-tortured bodies we confuse two graces: the dignity of self-belief and the courtesies of exchange. For us the ragged, untutored landscape seems as uncultured as our syntax.

So, like that folk choir, my first poems and plays expressed this yearning to be adopted, as the bastard longs

for his father's household. I saw myself legitimately prolonging the mighty line of Marlowe, of Milton, but my
sense of inheritance was stronger because it came from
estrangement. I would learn that every tribe hoards its culture as fiercely as its prejudices, that English literature,
even in the theatre, was hallowed ground and trespass,
that colonial literatures could grow to resemble it closely
but could never be considered its legitimate heir. There
was folk poetry, colonial poetry, Commonwealth verse,
etc., and their function, as far as their mother country was
concerned, was filial and tributary. I sighed up a continent
of envy when I studied English literature, yet, when I tried
to talk as I wrote, my voice sounded affected or too raw.
The tongue became burdened, like an ass trying to shift
its load. I was taught to trim my tongue as a particular
tool which could as easily have been ordered from England
as an awl or a chisel, and that eloquence which I required
of its actors was against the grain of their raw and innocent feeling. This kind of aggression increased an egotism
which can pass for genius. I was thus proclaimed a prodigy
because I insisted on a formality which had nothing to do
with their lives. It made me believe that twilight had set
me apart, and naturally I arrived at the heresy that landscape and history had failed me.

VIII

And in the end the age was handed
the sort of shit that it demanded.
—ERNEST HEMINGWAY

His defiance now a mania driven to the ptich where only
vision was real, the leader would pray: Let me help others
and be merciless to myself. But the torment of all self-
appointed schizoid saints is that they enact their opposite.

Thus, in his case also, strength of public purpose fed on private deterioration. So even righteous anger was corruptible; his self-sacrifice contained a fury that was really revenge. He alone would roll the Sisyphean boulder uphill, even if it cracked his backbone. The fuel of his ambition was no longer love but the ecstasy of nervous exhaustion and drink. This ecstasy, like all power, was heady, brutal, and corrupting. Its rages were forgiven because they were abstract, but every explosion eroded and demeaned the soul. He began to imagine treacheries where there was only misunderstanding. Nothing less than their self-blinded obedience would satisfy him. He had been warned of this madness, and true enough, paranoia progressed with every inch of slope cleared. But who would help should he let go of the stone, or, when he rested, help prop it with scotching heels and groaning back? On mornings of fitful remorse, after he had abused the actors, he would clinically study the symptoms: the blinding anger, the cirrhosis of suspicion, the heartsickness of failure. Perhaps these were the exactions of courage, but they left his skin prickling, his head roaring with amnesia, his ego massively inflamed. Such fury was suicidal. It had broken, even killed a few, but he saw each breakdown as revenge. Well, as they said in this country, who send him? There were fights with actors coarser than anything imaginable, where exasperation reduced to tears, whose violence annihilated all self-respect.

But even these explosions were better than the myth of the organic, ineradicable tsetse, the numbing fly in the mythically different blood, the myth of the uncreative, parasitic, malarial nigger, the marsh-numbed imagination that is happiest in mud. Anger was better than nothing, better than that embittered affection with which each called the other nigger. They moved from hall to basement to shed, and the parallel of all this was the cliché of the destitute, digs-deprived emigrant out on the grey streets; only this was supposed to be home, a launching place, a base of sorties and retreats from failure.

After a time invisible lianas strangle our will. Every night some area in the rapidly breeding bush of the mind would be cleared, an area where one could plan every inch of advance by firelight. Yes, the director was developing a Christ-complex, a readiness for suffering and betrayal, a Salvation Army theatre for the half-literate, the ambitious, the frustrated. What sustained him was a phrase from childhood—"Wherever two or three are gathered in Thy name"—and this increased in him, when only a handful of disciples showed up at rehearsals, an arrogant despair. It was more than a romance with the nobleness of failure, for his persistence was being complimented. One was now praised by those of one's generation who had given up art and whose realism comprised "integrity" and "public good," a new, brown meritocracy, who had accepted the limitations of their society, but whose solicitude concealed insult.

You had to endure their respect, their vapid, reassuring smiles at parties and at those dinners you were summoned to, to electrify with abuse. You went, knowing how dead they would be behind eyes that, repeated in the Sunday features, showed the nervous belligerence of graduates. They were eyes that denied their power, bright with charity. The idea of a theatre and the possibilities of their cities bored them, because they had accepted failure as logic. Duty had delineated itself to him—to transform the theatrical into theatre, to qualify the subtlety between a gift and a curse, but this was a society fed on an hysterical hallucination, that believed only the elaborate frenzy now controlled by the state. But Carnival was as meaningless as the art of the actor confined to mimicry. And now the intellectuals, courting and fearing the mass, found values

in it that they had formerly despised. They apotheosized
the folk form, insisting that calypsos were poems. Their
programme, for all its pretext to change, was a manual for
stasis, because they wanted politically to educate the peasant yet leave him intellectually unsoiled; they baffled him
with schisms and the complexities of Power while insisting
that he needed neither language nor logic, telling him that
what he yearned for was materialistic, imitative, and corrupt, while all his exhorters made sure that their wives
were white, their children brown, their jobs inviolate.

No, for the colonial artist the enemy was not the people, or the people's crude aesthetic, which he refined and
orchestrated; the enemy was those who had elected themselves as protectors of the people, frauds who cried out
against indignities done to the people, who urged them to
acquire pride, which meant abandoning their individual
dignity, who cried out that black was beautiful like trans-
mitters from a different revolution without explaining what
they meant by beauty, all of these had emerged from
nowhere suddenly, a different, startling "canaille." Their
rough philosophies were meant to coarsen every grace, to
demean courtesy, to brook no debate, their fury artificially
generated by an imitation of even metropolitan anger,
now. *Tristes, tristes tropiques!* We had come from an
older, wiser, sadder world that had already exorcised those
devils, but these were calling out the old devils to political
use. Witch doctors of the new left with imported totems.
The people were ready to be betrayed again.

So with fatigued conceit he realized that to continue
he would have to sustain the hallucination that the world
revolved around him. He lied to himself by cherishing
their devotion; he found not shame but promise in their
near-literacy, because he had accepted this role of martyr.
It gave him the perversity of remaining obscure while de-
siring fame, of being wrecked on a rock while hoping that

his whirlpool was the naval of the world. It was he who thought for them, who had salted their minds with subtleties that they might have been happier to ignore.

Exasperation nourished him. It urged him towards texts that were fantastical or violent, plays with the purgation of revenge. All he knew in those moods was that he wanted a theatre whose language could be that of the drowning, a gibberish of cries. It was fearful to carry that world within him alone. The contagion of that madness electrified them when they were all drunk or drunk on elation. Now he watched what he feared: the revolt that settles for security, the feeling in those still inadequate minds that they were message bearers. They might subjugate their bodies to everything, but every growth of power exposed their deficiencies. When they were excellent in gesture they were thick in speech, they could rarely explain or repeat what instinct clarified, and now a few would approach him with frightening requests: to understand the technique of theatre as if it were something different from what their bodies instinctually practiced, for better speech when theirs had vigour that was going out of English. Now they wanted to be as good as others. Good enough to go abroad. They showed that cursed, colonial hunger for the metropolis. The desertions had begun.

One does not lament the twenty years spent in trying to create this reality of a theatre, nor could one have contempt for its successes and the honours that "recognition" has brought, but the ceremony of reward is as misguided as the supposedly defunct system of long service, by which is meant self-sacrifice, for the reward itself acknowledges the odds which its donors have perpetuated by regarding art as monastic, by honouring the spirit after the body is worn down by the abrasions of indifference, by regarding the theatre as civic martyrdom. The theatre is a crass business, and money is better than medals. They thought in memorials, pensions, plaques. It is in that sense that nothing has changed, that one is still imprisoned in the fear of abandoning talent to despair. The messianic role is no longer flattering. It tires, it infuriates, it is sick of hearing "what would happen if . . ." It is not deceived by the noises of the state when it proclaims the power of folk culture, nor by the wily patronage of merchants. Without knowing it, the folk forms had become corrupted by politics. Their commercialization is now beyond anger, for they have become part of the climate, the art of the brochure.

:

What to do then? Where to turn? How to be true? If one went in search of the African experience, carrying the luggage of a few phrases and a crude map, where would it end? We had no language for the bush and there was a conflicting grammar in the pace of our movement. Out of this only an image came. A band of travellers, in their dim outlines like explorers who arrived at the crest of a dry, grassy ridge. There the air was heady, sharp, threading the lungs finely, with the view hidden, then levelling off to the tin-roofed, toy town of his childhood. The sense of hallucination increased with the actuality of every detail, from the chill, mildly shivering blades of hill grass, from their voices abrupted by the wind, the duality of time, past and present piercingly fixed as if the voluble puppets of his childhood were now frighteningly alive. A few pointed out the house with its pebbled back yard, where they had had their incarnations a quarter of a century ago, the roofs from which that martial cornet had struck its sparks, while some turned towards the lush, dark-pocketed valleys of banana with their ochre tracks and canted wooden huts, from whose kitchens, at firelight, the poetry which they spoke had come, and farther on, the wild, white-lined Atlantic coast with an Africa that was no longer home, and the dark, oracular mountain dying into mythology. It was as if, with this sinewy, tuned, elate company, he was repaying the island an ancestral debt. It was as if they had arrived at a view of their own bodies walking up the crest, their bodies tilted slightly forward, a few survivors. It was not a vision but a memory, though its detail was reduced, as in dreams and in art. But knowing the place could not tell me what it meant. There was only this reduced image of real actors on a real, windy grass ridge, which was, of course, the Morne overlooking the harbour of Castries and the banana fields to windward, on the very spine of St. Lucia. Perhaps it meant that I had brought us home. The cycle finished. Perhaps the ridge was a point of rest. Perhaps achievement. We would have to descend again. To leave that clear, heady air of achievement and go down again. I was with and not with them. I watched them but was not among them. They were they. They were there. They needed no more enthusiasm from the good guide, but for all the exhilaration of that air, I did not know where else to take them now, except up to the crest again, repeating the one image like a film. Henceforth no struggle, only the repetition of little victories. Had one closed their hopes or opened them? There was a value in darkness, in the cultivation of obscurity. On that little summit, where the air is spring-nipped or autumn-chilling, I may have lost them.

The last image is of a rain-flushed dawn, after a back-breaking night of filming, in a slowly greying field where the sea wind is like metal on the cheek. In the litter of the field, among black boxes of equipment and yellow, sleekly wet tarpaulins, stands a shawled girl caught in that gesture which abstractedly gathers cloth to shoulder, her black hair lightly lifting, the tired, pale skin flushed, lost in herself and the breaking camp. She was white, and that no longer mattered. Her stillness annihilated years of anger. His heart thanked her silently from the depth of exhaustion, for she was one of a small army of his dreams. She was a vessel caught at the moment of departure of their Muse, her clear vacancy the question of a poem

which is its own answer. She was among the sentries who
had watched till dawn.

I am bound within them, neither knowing which is
liana or trunk, which is the parasite, which is the host,
since if I dared to confess to ambition I could be using
them, and they the same. All their betrayals are quarrels
with the self, their pardonable desertions the inevitable
problem of all island artists: the choice of home or exile,
self-realization or spiritual betrayal of one's country.
Travelling widens this breach. Choice grows more melodramatic with every twilight. When twenty years ago we
imagined cities devoted neither to power nor to money but
to art, one had the true vision. Everything else has been
the sweated blurring of a mirror in which the people might
have found their true reflection.

(1970)

The Muse of History

History is the nightmare from which I am trying to awake.
—JOYCE

I

The common experience of the New World, even for its patrician writers whose veneration of the Old is read as the idolatry of the mestizo, is colonialism. They, too, are victims of tradition, but they remind us of our debt to the great dead, that those who break a tradition first hold it in awe. They perversely encourage disfavour, but because their sense of the past is of a timeless, yet habitable, moment, the New World owes them more than it does those who wrestle with that past, for their veneration subtilizes an arrogance which is tougher than violent rejection. They know that by openly fighting tradition we perpetuate it, that revolutionary literature is a filial impulse, and that maturity is the assimiliation of the features of every ancestor.

When these writers cunningly describe themselves as classicists and pretend an indifference to change, it is with an irony as true of the colonial anguish as the fury of the radical. If they appear to be phony aristocrats, it is because they have gone past the confrontation of history, that Medusa of the New World.

These writers reject the idea of history as time for its original concept as myth, the partial recall of the race. For them history is fiction, subject to a fitful muse, memory. Their philosophy, based on a contempt for historic time, is revolutionary, for what they repeat to the New World is its simultaneity with the Old. Their vision of man is elemental, a being inhabited by presences, not a creature chained to his past. Yet the method by which we are taught the past, the progress from motive to event, is the same by which we read narrative fiction. In time every event becomes an exertion of memory and is thus subject to invention. The further the facts, the more history petrifies into myth. Thus, as we grow older as a race, we grow aware that history is written, that it is a kind of literature without morality, that in its actuaries the ego of the race is indissoluble and that everything depends on whether we write this fiction through the memory of hero or of victim.

In the New World servitude to the muse of history has produced a literature of recrimination and despair, a literature of revenge written by the descendants of slaves or a literature of remorse written by the descendants of masters. Because this literature serves historical truth, it yellows into polemic or evaporates in pathos. The truly tough aesthetic of the New World neither explains nor forgives history. It refuses to recognize it as a creative or culpable force. This shame and awe of history possess poets of the Third World who think of language as enslavement and who, in a rage for identity, respect only incoherence or nostalgia.

II

The great poets of the New World, from Whitman to Neruda, reject this sense of history. Their vision of man in the New World is Adamic. In their exuberance he is still

capable of enormous wonder. Yet he has paid his accounts
to Greece and Rome and walks in a world without mon-
uments and ruins. They exhort him against the fearful
magnet of older civilizations. Even in Borges, where the
genius seems secretive, immured from change, it celebrates an elation which is vulgar and abrupt, the life of
the plains given an instant archaism by the hieratic style.
Violence is felt with the simultaneity of history. So the
death of a gaucho does not merely repeat, but is, the death
of Caesar. Fact evaporates into myth. This is not the jaded
cynicism which sees nothing new under the sun, it is an
elation which sees everything as renewed. Like Borges,
too, the poet St.-John Perse conducts us from the mythology of the past to the present without a tremor of ad-
justment. This is the revolutionary spirit at its deepest; it
recalls the spirit to arms. In Perse there is the greatest
width of elemental praise of winds, seas, rains. The revolutionary or cyclic vision is as deeply rooted as the patrician syntax. What Perse glorifies is not veneration but the
perennial freedom; his hero remains the wanderer, the
man who moves through the ruins of great civilizations
with all his worldly goods by caravan or pack mule, the
poet carrying entire cultures in his head, bitter perhaps,
but unencumbered. His are poems of massive or solitary
migrations through the elements. They are the same in
spirit as the poems of Whitman or Neruda, for they seek
spaces where praise of the earth is ancestral.

III

New World poets who see the "classic style" as stasis must
see it also as historical degradation, rejecting it as the language of the master. This self-torture arises when the poet
also sees history as language, when he limits his memory
to the suffering of the victim. Their admirable wish to honour the degraded ancestor limits their language to pho-

netic pain, the groan of suffering, the curse of revenge. The tone of the past becomes an unbearable burden, for they must abuse the master or hero in his own language, and this implies self-deceit. Their view of Caliban is of the enraged pupil. They cannot separate the rage of Caliban from the beauty of his speech when the speeches of Caliban are equal in their elemental power to those of his tutor. The language of the torturer mastered by the victim. This is viewed as servitude, not as victory.

:

But who in the New World does not have a horror of the past, whether his ancestor was torturer or victim? Who, in the depth of conscience, is not silently screaming for pardon or for revenge? The pulse of New World history is the racing pulse beat of fear, the tiring cycles of stupidity and greed. The tongues above our prayers utter the pain of entire races to the darkness of a Manichean God: *Dominus illuminatio mea*, for what was brought to this New World under the guise of divine light, the light of the sword blade and the light of *dominus illuminatio mea*, was the same iridescent serpent brought by a contaminating Adam, the same tortured Christ exhibited with Christian exhaustion, but what was also brought in the seeded entrails of the slave was a new nothing, a darkness which intensified the old faith.

In time the slave surrendered to amnesia. That amnesia is the true history of the New World. That is our inheritance, but to try and understand why this happened, to condemn or justify is also the method of history, and these explanations are always the same: This happened because of that, this was understandable because, and in days men were such. These recriminations exchanged, the contrition of the master replaces the vengeance of the slave, and here colonial literature is most pietistic, for it can accuse great art of feudalism and excuse poor art as suffering. To radical poets poetry seems the homage of

resignation, an essential fatalism. But it is not the pressure
of the past which torments great poets but the weight of
the present:

> there are so many dead,
> and so many dikes the red sun breached,
> and so many heads battering hulls
> and so many hands that have closed over kisses
> and so many things that I want to forget.

—PABLO NERUDA

The sense of history in poets lives rawly along their nerves:

> My land without name, without America,
> equinoctial stamen, lance-like purple,
> your aroma rose through my roots
> into the cup I drained, into the most tenuous
> word not yet born in my mouth.

—PABLO NERUDA

It is this awe of the numinous, this elemental privilege of
naming the New World which annihilates history in our
great poets, an elation common to all of them, whether
they are aligned by heritage to Crusoe and Prospero or to
Friday and Caliban. They reject ethnic ancestry for faith
in elemental man. The vision, the "democratic vista," is
not metaphorical, it is a social necessity. A political philosophy rooted in elation would have to accept belief in a
second Adam, the re-creation of the entire order, from
religion to the simplest domestic rituals. The myth of the
noble savage would not be revived, for that myth never
emanated from the savage but has always been the nostalgia of the Old World, its longing for innocence. The
great poetry of the New World does not pretend to such

innocence, its vision is not naïve. Rather, like its fruits, its savour is a mixture of the acid and the sweet, the apples of its second Eden have the tartness of experience. In such poetry there is a bitter memory and it is the bitterness that dries last on the tongue. It is the acidulous that supplies its energy. The golden apples of this sun are shot with acid. The taste of Neruda is citric, the *Pomme de Cythère* of Aimé Césaire sets the teeth on edge, the savour of Perse is of salt fruit at the sea's edge, the sea grape, the "fat-poke," the sea almond. For us in the archipelago the tribal memory is salted with the bitter memory of migration.

:

To such survivors, to all the decimated tribes of the New World who did not suffer extinction, their degraded arrival must be seen as the beginning, not the end, of our history. The shipwrecks of Crusoe and of the crew in *The Tempest* are the end of an Old World. It should matter nothing to the New World if the Old is again determined to blow itself up, for an obsession with progress is not within the psyche of the recently enslaved. That is the bitter secret of the apple. The vision of progress is the rational madness of history seen as sequential time, of a dominated future. Its imagery is absurd. In the history books the discoverer sets a shod food on virgin sand, kneels, and the savage also kneels from his bushes in awe. Such images are stamped on the colonial memory, such heresy as the world's becoming holy from Crusoe's footprint or the imprint of Columbus's knee. These blasphemous images fade, because these hieroglyphs of progress are basically comic. And if the idea of the New and the Old becomes increasingly absurd, what must happen to our sense of time, what else can happen to history itself, but that it, too, is becoming absurd? This is not existentialism. Adamic, elemental man cannot be existential. His first impulse is not self-indulgence but awe, and existentialism is simply the myth of the noble savage gone baroque. Such philosophies of freedom are born in cities. Existentialism is as much nostalgia as in Rousseau's sophisticated primitivism, as sick as recurrence in French thought as the isle of Cythera, whether it is the tubercular, fevered imagery of Watteau or the same fever turned delirious in Rimbaud and Baudelaire. The poets of the "New Aegean," of the Isles of the Blest, the Fortunate Isles, of the remote Bermudas, of Prospero's isle, of Crusoe's Juan Fernandez, of Cythera, of all those rocks named like the beads of a chaplet, they know that the old vision of Paradise wrecks here.

> *I want to hear a song in which the rainbow breaks*
> *and the curlew alights among forgotten shores*
> *I want the liana creeping on the palm-tree*
> *(on the trunk of the present 'tis our stubborn future)*
> *I want the conquistador with unsealed armour*
> *lying down in death of perfumed flowers,*
> *the foam censing a sword gone rusty*
> *in the pure blue flight of slow wild cactuses*

—AIMÉ CÉSAIRE

But to most writers of the archipelago who contemplate only the shipwreck, the New World offers not elation but cynicism, a despair at the vices of the Old which they feel must be repeated. Their malaise is an oceanic nostalgia for the older culture and a melancholy at the new, and this can go as deep as a rejection of the untamed landscape, a yearning for ruins. To such writers the death of civilizations is architectural, not spiritual; seeded in their memories is an imagery of vines ascending broken columns, of dead terraces, of Europe as a nourishing museum. They believe in the responsibility of tradition, but what they are in awe of is not tradition, which is alert, alive, simultaneous, but history, and the same is true of the new magnifiers of Africa. For these their deepest loss is of the old gods, the fear that it is worship which has enslaved progress. Thus the humanism of politics replaces religion. They see such gods as part of the process of history, subjected like the tribe to cycles of achievement and despair. Because the Old World concept of God is anthropomorphic, the New World slave was forced to remake himself in His image, despite such phrases as "God is light, and in Him is no darkness," and at this point of intersecting faiths the enslaved poet and enslaved priest surrendered their power. But the tribe in bondage learned to fortify itself by cunning assimilation of the religion of the Old World. What seemed to be surrender was redemption. What seemed the loss of tradition was its renewal. What seemed the death of faith was its rebirth.

IV

Eliot speaks of the culture of a people as being the incarnation of its religion. If this is true, in the New World we have to ask this faceted question: (1) Whether the religion taught to the black slave has been absorbed as belief, (2) whether it has been altered by this absorption, and (3) whether wholly absorbed or absorbed and altered, it must now be rejected. In other terms, can an African culture exist, except on the level of polemical art or politics, without an African religion, and if so, which African religion?

The spectacle of mediocre talents raising old totems is more shameful than the faith of the convert which they ridicule, but the flare of a literary religion is brief, for faith needs more than style. At this stage the polemic poet, like the politician, will wish to produce epic work, to summon the grandeur of the past, not as myth but as history, and to prophesy in the way that Fascist architecture can be viewed as prophesy. Yet the more ambitious the zeal, the more diffuse and forced it becomes, the more it roots into

research, until the imagination surrenders to the glorification of history, the ear becomes enslaved, the glorifiers of
the tom-tom ignoring the dynamo. These epic poets create
an artificial past, a defunct cosmology without the tribal
faith.

What remains in the archipelago is the fragmenta-
tion into schisms, the private cosmology of the wayside
preacher. Every day in these islands the sidewalk blossoms
with such victims, minds disfigured by their attempt to
comprehend both worlds unless they create a heaven of
which they are the centre. Like the wayside prophets, the
"epic" poet in the islands looks to anthropology, to a catalogue of forgotten gods, to midden fragments, artifacts,
and the unfinished phrases of a dead speech. These engage in masochistic recollection. The epic-minded poet
looks around these islands and finds no ruins, and because
all epic is based on the visible presence of ruins, wind-
bitten or sea-bitten, the poet celebrates what little there
is, the rusted slave wheel of the sugar factory, cannon,
chains, the crusted amphora of cutthroats, all the para-
phernalia of degradation and cruelty which we exhibit as
history, not as masochism, as if the ovens of Auschwitz
and Hiroshima were the temples of the race. Morbidity is
the inevitable result, and that is the tone of any literature
which respects such a history and bases its truth on shame
or on revenge.

And yet it is there that the epic poetry of the tribe
originates, in its identification with Hebraic suffering, the
migration, the hope of deliverance from bondage. There
was this difference, that the passage over our Red Sea was
not from bondage to freedom but its opposite, so that the
tribes arrived at their New Canaan chained. There is this
residual feeling in much of our literature, the wailing by
strange waters for a lost home. It survives in our politics,
the subdued search for a Moses. The epic concept was
compressed in the folk lyric, the mass longing in chanter

and chorus, couplet and refrain. The revivalist poems drew their strength from the self-hypnotic nature of their responses, interminable in monody as the tribal hope.

> *I know moonrise, I know star-rise,*
> *Lay this body down,*
> *I go to my Lord in the evening of the day,*
> *Lay this body down.*

But this monody is not only resigned but martial:

> *Joshua fit de battle of Jericho,*
> *Jericho, Jericho,*
> *Joshua fit de battle of Jericho,*
> *And the walls come tumbling down.*

The epic poem is not a literary project. It is already written; it was written in the mouths of the tribe, a tribe which had courageously yielded its history.

v

While the Old Testament epics of bondage and deliverance provided the slave with a political parallel, the ethics of Christianity tempered his vengeance and appeared to deepen his passivity. To his masters this world was not new but an extension of the old. Their vision of an earthly Paradise was denied him, and the reward offered in the name of Christian suffering would come after his death. All this we know, but the phenomenon is the zeal with which the slave accepted both the Christian and the Hebraic, resigned his gaze to the death of his pantheon, and yet deliberately began to invest a decaying faith with a political belief. Historians cannot chronicle this, except they go by the statistics of conversion. There is no moment of a mass tribal conversion equal to the light's unhorsing of Saul; what we were told to believe instead was a slow, massive groan of surrender, the immense laborious conversion of the defeated into good niggers, or true Christians; and certainly songs such as this one seem to be the most contemptible expression of the beaten:

> I'm going to lay down my sword and shield,
> Down by the riverside, down by the riverside . . .
>
> I ain't going study war no more,
> Study war no more . . .

How can we teach this as history? Aren't those the words of the whitewashed, the defeated, isn't this the Christian treachery that seduces revenge, that led the exhausted tribes to betray their gods? A new generation looks back on such conversion with contempt, for where are the songs of triumph, the defiance of the captured warrior, where are the nostalgic battle chants and the seasonal songs of harvest, the seeding of the great African pastoral? This generation sees in the epic poetry of the work song and the early blues self-contempt and inertia, but the deep truth is that pinioned and humiliated in body as the slave was, there is, beyond simple fortitude, a note of aggression, and what a later generation sees as defeat is really the willing of spiritual victory, for the captured warrior and the tribal poet had chosen the very battleground which the captor proposed, the soul:

> I am a warrior, out in the field,
> And I can sing, and I can shout,
> And I can tell it all about that Jesus died for me,
> When I get over yonder in the happy paradise,
> When I get over yonder in the field.

What was captured from the captor was his God, for the subject African had come to the New World in an elemental intimacy with nature, with a profounder terror of blasphemy than the exhausted, hypocritical Christian. He understood too quickly the Christian rituals of a whipped, tortured, and murdered redeemer, though he may have recoiled at dividing and eating his flesh, for in primal cultures gods defeat each other like warriors, and for warriors there is no conversion in defeat. There are many such warriors in the history of the archipelago, but the true history is of the tribe's conversion, and it is this which is our concern. It returns us to Eliot's pronouncement, that a culture cannot exist without a religion, and to other pronouncements irradiating that idea, that an epic poetry cannot exist without a religion. It is the beginning of the poetry of the New World. And the language used is, like the religion, that of the conqueror of the God. But the slave had wrested God from his captor.

In tribal, elemental poetry, the epic experience of the race is compressed in metaphor. In an oral tradition the mode is simple, the response open-ended, so that each new poet can add his lines to the form, a process very much like weaving or the dance, based on the concept that the history of the tribe is endless. There is no dying fall, no egotistical signature of effect; in short, no pathos. The blues is not pathos, not the individual voice, it is a tribal mode, and each new oral poet can contribute his couplet, and this is based on the concept that the tribe, inured to despair, will also survive: there is no beginning but no end. The new poet enters a flux and withdraws, as the weaver continues the pattern, hand to hand and mouth to mouth, as the rockpile convict passes the sledge:

> *Many days of sorrow, many nights of woe,*
> *Many days of sorrow, many nights of woe,*
> *And a ball and chain, everywhere I go.*

No history, but flux, and the only sustenance, myth:

> *Moses lived till he got old,*
> *Where shall I be?*

The difference is in the intensity of celebration. The pietistic rhythm of the missionary is speeded to a martial frenzy which the slave adapts to a triumphal tribal mode. Good, the missionary and merchant must have thought, once we've got them swinging and clapping, all will be peace, but their own God was being taken away from merchant and missionary by a submerged force that rose at ritual gatherings, where the subconscious rhythm rose and took possession and where, in fact, the Hebraic-European God was changing colour, for the names of the sub-deities did not matter, Saint Ursula or Saint Urzulie; the Catholic pantheon adapted easily to African pantheism. Catholic mystery adapted easily to African magic. Not all accepted the white man's God. As prologue to the Haitian revolution, Boukman was invoking Damballa in the Bois Cayman. Blood sacrifices, warrior initiations, tortures, escapes, revolts, even the despair of slaves who went mad and ate dirt, these are the historical evidence, but what is finally important is that the race or the tribes were converted, they became Christian. But no race is converted against its will. The slave master now encountered a massive pliability. The slave converted himself, he changed weapons, spiritual weapons, and as he adapted his master's religion, he also adapted his language, and it is here that what we can look at as our poetic tradition begins. Now began the new naming of things.

Epic was compressed in the folk legend. The act of imagination was the creative effort of the tribe. Later such legends may be written by individual poets, but their beginnings are oral, familial, the poetry of firelight which illuminates the faces of a tight, primal hierarchy. But even oral literature forces itself towards hieroglyph and alphabet. Today, still in many islands, the West Indian poet is faced with a language which he hears but cannot write because there are no symbols for such a language and because the closer he brings hand and word to the precise inflections of the inner language and to the subtlest accuracies of his ear, the more chaotic his symbols will appear on the page, the smaller the regional dialect, the more eccentric his representation of it will become, so his function remains the old one of being filter and purifier, never losing the tone and strength of the common speech as he uses the hieroglyphs, symbols, or alphabet of the official one. Now two of the greatest poets of this archipelago have come from French-patois-speaking islands. St.-John Perse, born and reared until late adolescence in Guadeloupe, and Aimé Césaire, the Martiniquan. Both have the colonial experience of language, one from privilege, the other from deprivation. Let it not be important for now that one is white, the other black. Both are Frenchmen, both are poets who write in French. Well, to begin with, it is Césaire's language which is the more abstruse, more difficult, more surrealist, while Perse's French is classic. Césaire has not written his great poem, *Cahier d'un retour au pays natal*, in dialect, but we must pay attention to its tone. For all the complexity of its surrealism, its sometimes invented words, it sounds, to at least one listener familiar with French patois, like a poem written tonally in Creole. Those tonal qualities are tartness and impatience, but the language of Césaire in this great revolutionary poem, or rather a poem partially appropriated by revolutionaries, is not proletarian. The tone of Perse is also majestic, it marches a path of inevitable conquest appropriating as it proceeds; and to the reader trying to listen purely to the language of either poet without prejudice, without subliminal whispers of history, they have at least one thing in common: authority. Their diction has other similarities, for instance, form. In *Cahier d'un retour au pays natal*, as well as in the prose poems of Perse from the Antillean *Eloges* to *Chronique* and beyond, there is a strict, synonymous armature shared within the tradition of the metropolitan language, and which both must have felt to be an inheritance despite their racial and social differences, despite the distance of Perse from the dialect of house servants and of fishermen, despite the fealty of Césaire to that dialect. The sources of that diction are both ancient and contemporary: the Bible and the tribal ode as well as French surrealist poetry, the proletarian hymns of Whitman, and the oral or written legends of other civilizations, for Perse the East and the Mediterranean, for Césaire the Hebraic Mediterranean and Africa. In visual structure the poetry of both shares the symmetry of the prose ode, the appearance of translation from an older epic which invests their poems with an air of legend. Now here are two colonials or, more precisely, two poets whose formative perceptions, whose apprehension of the visible worlds of their very different childhoods, were made numinous by their elation in the metropolitan language, and whose very different visions created indisputable masterpieces, and, here is the point, without doing violence to the language itself, in fact perpetuating its grandeur through opposite beliefs, Perse through prophesy and nostalgia, Césaire through nostalgia and polemic. Yet, as a translator, I would rather attempt an equivalent in English to Perse than to Césaire, for the simple reason that Perse is perhaps simpler, for where his language grows abstruse in the vocabularies of archaeology, marine biology, botany, and so forth, the language of Césaire skims the subtleties of modern surrealism. Yet as an Antillean, I feel more akin to Césaire's tone.

I do not know if one poet is indebted to the other, but whatever the bibliographical truth is, one acknowl-

edges not an exchange of influences, not imitation, but
the tidal advance of the metropolitan language, of its empire, if you like, which carries simultaneously, fed by such
strong colonial tributaries, poets of such different beliefs
as Rimbaud, Char, Claudel, Perse, and Césaire. It is the
language which is the empire, and great poets are not its
vassals but its princes. We continue to categorize these
poets by the wrong process; that is, by history. We continue to fiddle with the obvious limitations of dialect because of chauvinism, but the great poem of Césaire's could
not be written in a French Creole dialect because there
are no words for some of its concepts; there are no equivalent nouns for its objects, and because even if these were
suddenly found, they could not be visually expressed without the effort of an insane philologist. Both poets manip-
ulate a supreme, visionary rhetoric that carries over into
English. Sometimes they sound identical:

1. *Narrow path of the surge in the blur of fables . . .*
   —CÉSAIRE

2. *Wandering, what did we know of our ancestral bed, all*
   blazoned
   though it were in that speckled wood of the Islands? . . .
   There
   was no name for us in the ancient bronze gong of the old
   family house. There was no name for us in our mother's
   oratory
   (jacaranda wood or cedar), nor in the golden antennae
   quivering
   in the head-dresses of our guardians, women of colour. We
   were
   not in the lute-maker's wood, in the spinet or the harp:
   nor . . .
   —PERSE

3. *I want to hear a song in which the rainbow breaks*
   and the curlew alights along forgotten shores
   I want the liana creeping on the palm-tree
   (on the trunk of the present 'tis our stubborn future)
   I want the conquistador with unsealed armour
   lying down in death of perfumed flowers,
   the foam censing a sword gone rusty
   in the pure blue flight of slow wild cactuses.
   —CÉSAIRE

4. *Master of the three roads a man stands before you who*
   walked much,
   Master of the three roads a man stands before you
   who walked on hands who walked on feet who
   walked on the belly who walked on the
   behind.
   Since Elam. Since Akkad. Since Sumer.
   Master of the three roads a man stands before you who
   has carried much.
   And truly, friends, I carried since Elam, since Akkad, since
   Sumer.
   —CÉSAIRE

Perse and Césaire, men of diametrically challenging backgrounds, racial opposites, to use the language of politics, one patrician and conservative, the other proletarian and revolutionary, classic and romantic, Prospero and Caliban, all such opposites balance easily, but they balance on the axis of a shared sensibility, and this sensibility, with or deprived of the presence of a visible tradition, is the sensibility of walking to a New World. Perse sees in this New World vestiges of the Old, of order and of hierarchy, Césaire sees in it evidence of past humiliations and the need for a new order, but the deeper truth is that both poets perceive this New World through mystery. Their language tempts us to endless quotation; there are moments when one hears both voices simultaneously, until the tone is one voice from these different men. If we think of one as poor and the other as privileged when we read their addresses to the New World, if we must see one as black and one as white, we are not only dividing this sensibility by the process of the sociologist, we are denying the range of either poet, the power of compassion and the power of fury. One is not making out a case for assimilation and for the common simplicity of all men; we are interested in their differences, openly, but what astonishes us in both poets is their elation, their staggering elation in possibility. And one is not talking of a possible ideal society, for you will find that only in the later work of Perse, a society which is inaccessible by its very grandeur, but of the elation in presences which exists in *Éloges* and in *Pour fêter une enfance*, the possibility of the individual Caribbean man, African, European, or Asian in ancestry, the enormous, gently opening morning of his possibility, his body touched with dew, his nerves as subtilized to sensation as the mimosa, his memory, whether of grandeur or of pain, gradually erasing itself as recurrent drizzles cleanse the ancestral or tribal markings from the coral skull, the possibility of a man and his language waking to wonder here. As the language of Perse later becomes hammered and artificial, so does the rhetoric of Césaire move towards the heraldic, but their first great work is as deeply rooted and supple as a vine.

But these poems are in French. The fact that they have now begun to influence English poetry from the archipelago is significant, because they are powerful works and all power attracts to itself, but their rhetoric is unmanageable for our minor "revolutionary" poets, who assume a grandeur without a language to create it, for these imitators see both poems through history, or through sociology; they are seduced by their subjects. Therefore, there is now a brood of thin, querulous fledglings who steal fragments of Césaire for their own nests, and yet these fledglings will condemn Perse as a different animal, a white poet. These convulsions of bad poetry appear when the society is screaming for change.

Because we think of tradition as history, one group of anatomists claims that this tradition is wholly African and that its responses are alerted through the nostalgia of one race, but that group must allow the Asian and the Mediterranean the same fiction, and then the desolate terraces of Perse's epic memory will be as West Indian to the Middle Easterners among us as the kingdoms of the Guinea coast are to Césaire or the poetry of China is to the Chinese grocer. If we can psychologize, divide, trace these degenerations easily, then we must accept the miracle of possibility which every poet demonstrates. The Caribbean sensibility is not marinated in the past. It is not exhausted. It is new. But it is its complexity, not its historically explained simplicities, which is new. Its traces of melancholy are the chemical survivals of the blood which remain after the slave's and the indentured worker's convalescence. It will survive the malaria of nostalgia and the delirium of revenge, just as it survived its self-contempt.

Thus, while many critics of contemporary Commonwealth verse reject imitation, the basis of the tradition, for originality, the false basis of innovation, they represent eventually the old patronizing attitude adapted to contemporaneous politics, for their demand for naturalness, novelty, originality, or truth is again based on preconceptions of behaviour. They project reflexes as anticipated as the exuberance, spontaneity, and refreshing dialect of the tribe. Certain performances are called for, including the fashionable incoherence of revolutionary anger, and everyone is again appeased, the masochist critic by the required attack on his "values," the masochist poet by the approval of his victim. Minstrel postures, in their beginnings, are hard to identify from private truths, but their familiarity soon establishes the old formulae of entertainment. Basically, the anger of the black is entertainment or theater, if it makes an aesthetic out of anger, and this is no different in its "naturalness" than the legendary joy or spontaneous laughter of the minstrel. It is still nightclub and cabaret, professional fire-eating and dancing on broken bottles. The critic-tourist can only gasp at such naturalness. He wouldn't care to try it himself, really. We are back to Dr. Johnson's female preacher.

The liberal warms to the speech of the ghetto in a way quite contemptible to the poet, for the benignity of the liberal critic perpetuates the sociological conditions of that speech, despite his access to anger. What he really preaches again, but this time through criticism, is the old separate-but-equal argument. Blacks are different, and the pathos is that most blacks have been led to believe this, and into the tragedy of proclaiming their difference. The theories clash, for the radical seeks to equate the deprived up to the status of the privileged, while the liberal and his unconscious accomplices, the poets of the ghetto and of "revolutionary rhetoric," fear to lose "their own thing" if they let thought and education widen by materialist benefits. Often it is the educated and privileged poet who masks his education and privilege behind a fake exoticism of poverty and the pastoral. They write one way and speak another. There has been the treason of clerks, and now we have the treason of the intellectuals.

The degeneration of technique, when technique is an open question, hides itself in originality. Bad verse written by blacks is better than good verse written by whites, because, say the revolutionaries, the same standards do not apply. This is seen as pride, as the opposite of inferiority. So too, one can isolate in this writer's general demeanor of style that belligerent naïveté or a joy unqualified which characterizes a pubescent literature. One which accepts subconsciously a condition of being praised or corrected, which may resist, but also insinuates by resistance, the correctives of a "superior" or at least an older discipline or tradition. It is a flaw which also sees history as a ladder of achievement, but it is a competitive energy which either fails often from exhaustion or amazes by its prolixity. It is manic, it is inferior, but it is certain of its direction and challenges. It engages its peers. For purity, then, for pure black Afro-Aryanism, only the unsoiled black is valid, and West Indianism is a taint, and other strains adulterate him. The extremists, the purists, are beginning to exercise those infections, so that a writer of "mixed," hence "degenerate," blood can be nothing stronger than a liberal. This will develop a rich individualism through a deeper bitterness, it will increase egocentricity and isolation, because such writers and poets already have more complex values. They will seem more imperialistic, nostalgic, and out of the impetus of the West Indian proletariat, because they cannot simplify intricacies of race and the thought of the race. They will become hermits or rogue animals, increasingly exotic hybrids, broken bridges between two ancestries, Europe and the Third World of Africa and Asia; in other words, they will become islands. Because of this isolation their ironic fate will be to appear inaccessible, irrelevant, remote. The machinery of radicalism which makes culture heroes of more violent writers and which makes a virtue of immediacy will not include them. They are condemned to middle age.

And all of this has sprung, at the root, from a rejection of language. The new cult of incoherence, of manic repetition, glorifies the apprentice, and it also atrophies the young, who are warned against assimilation. It is as if the instinct of the black is still escape, escape to the labyrinth, escape to a special oblivion removed from the banalties of poverty and from the weight of a new industrial imperialism, that of absentee "power structures" which control the archipelago's economy. That there will always be abrupt eruptions of defiance is almost irrelevant itself, because the impulse of such eruptions, their political philosophy, remains simplistic and shallow. That all blacks are beautiful is an enervating statement, that all blacks are brothers more a reprimand than a charter, that the people must have power almost their death wish, for the real power of this time is silent. Art cannot last long in this shale. It crumbles like those slogans, fragments and shards of a historical fault. Power now becomes increasingly divided and tribal when it is based on genetics. It leads to the righteous secondary wars of the Third World, to the self-maiming of civil wars, the frontier divisions of third-rate, Third World powers, manipulated or encouraged by the first powers. Genocides increase, tribal wars increase and become increasingly hallucinatory and remote. Nigeria, Bangladesh, Vietnam, the Middle East, Greece, the Spains of our era. The provincial revolutions can only spare a general compassion because they know who manages or stages such things. They believe that the same manipulation is beneath them.

The revolution is here. It was always here. It does not need the decor of African tourism or the hip postures and speech of metropolitan ghettos. Change the old word "slum" for the new word "ghetto" and you have the psychology of funk, a market psychology that, within a year of the physical revolution, has been silently appropriated by Mediterranean and Asian merchants. Soul is a commodity. Soul is an outfit. The "metropolitan" emphasis of the "revolution" has clouded the condition of the peasant, of the inevitably rooted man, and the urban revolutionary is by imitation or by nature rootless and a drifter, fashionably so, and in time a potential exile. The peasant cannot spare himself these city changes. He is the true African who does not need to proclaim it.

ON HISTORY AS EXILE

Postures of metropolitan cynicism must be assumed by the colonial in exile if he is not to feel lost, unless he prefers utter isolation or the desperate, noisy nostalgia of fellow exiles. This cynicism is an attempt to enter the sense of history which is within every Englishman and European, but which he himself has never felt towards Africa or Asia. There develops the other sense, that the history of Africa or of Asia is inferior, and we see how close we draw to madness here, for this sense qualifies not the significance of an event but the event itself, the action of the event as second class. The exile will not be argued out of this. He has chosen to see history this way, and that is his vision. The simplifications of imperialism, of the colonial heritage, are more dignified, for these gave brutish tribes their own dignity. But even less honest than the colonial in exile is the generation after him, which wants to effect a eugenic leap from imperialism to independence by longing for the ancestral dignity of the wanderer-warrior. Mysterious customs. Defunct gods. Sacred rites. As much as the colonial, however, they are children of the nineteenth-century ideal, the romance of redcoat and savage warrior, their simplification of choosing to play Indian instead of cowboy, filtered through films and adolescent literature, is the hallucination of imperial romance; the posture is melodramatic, the language of its stances idealized from the literature of exploration remembered from Captain Marryat, Kipling, or Rider Haggard. It continues the juvenile romance of savage drums, tribal rites, barbarous but sacred sacrifices, golden journeys, lost cities. In the subconscious there is a black Atlantis buried in a sea of sand.

The colonial is tougher. He sees history for what it is in the world around him, an almost inexpressible banality.

He sees the twentieth century without self-deceit and juvenile fantasy. The other curses the banality and chooses
myth. Poets of the second group now begin to see poetry
as a form of historical instruction. Their target is the of-
ficialized literature of the schools, the sociologists, their
fellow historians, and, above all, the revolution. They become fascinated with the efficacy of poetry as an aspect
of power not through its language but through its subject.
Their poetry becomes a kind of musical accompaniment
to certain theses, and as history it is forced to exclude
certain contradictions, for history cannot be ambiguously
recorded. Whatever its motive, either this happened or it
did not. All piety is seen as villainy, all form as hypocrisy.

Inevitably, these poets grow obsessed with the innovation of forms, but this innovation is seen as critical strategy, for it will need to attack others as well as defend its
position, if it is to be seen as spontaneous choice. Con-
servatively, it imitates what it believes to be the tribal
mode, and it makes no distinction between the artificiality
of the high style of tribal ceremony and the language
which it employs to achieve this. It may even use fragments of the original language to adorn itself, even if such
language is not its natural tongue. A new conservatism
now appears, a new dignity more reactionary and pompous
than the direction of the language used. It moves mani-
cally between the easy applause of dialect, the argot of the
tribe and ceremonial speech, the "memory" of the tribe;
that is, between the new dignity and the popular, and in
between there is nothing. The normal voice of the poet,
his own speaking voice is lost, and no language is writ.

No, if we look for the primal imagination in West
Indian literature, its "revolutionary" aspect, we find it cru-
cially evolving in West Indian fiction, the poetic principle
is more alert in our best prose, and whatever ethnic impulse drives this imagination examines the roots of con-

temporary man with the same force as poets of a different race using English. In the Guyanese novelist Denis Williams's *Other Leopards* there is this passage:

Now, having removed my body and the last traces of it, I am without context clear. Going up this new tree, picking the thorns bare, one by one, I am in a darkness nowhere at all, I am nothing, nowhere. This is something gained. Hughie has not found me; I have outwitted him. I have achieved a valuable state: a condition outside his method. Only remains now to remove my consciousness. This I can do whenever I wish. I am free of the earth. I do not need to go down there for anything.

In "Wodwo" by Ted Hughes there is:

> *What am I? nosing here turning leaves over*
> *following a faint stain on the air to the river's edge*
> *I enter water . . .*
> > *I seem*
> *separate from the ground not rooted but dropped*
> *out of nothing casually I've not threads*
> *fastening me to anything I can go anywhere*
> *I seem to have been given the freedom*
> *of this place what am I then . . .*

which, excuse the broken quotations, is the tone of the whole poem, language, tone, hesitation, and assurance, the deliberate picking out of names, the numinous process in Williams of a man reduced, in Hughes of a man evolving, the passage from the novel and the whole of Hughes's poem are the same. They are not merely the same in subject, anthropology; in fact, they are different in structure obviously, and there is absolutely no question of exchanged influences except Hughes had read Williams, whose book appeared some years before, but what is there is the displaced, searching psyche of modern man, the reversion of twentieth-century man, whether in Africa or in Yorkshire, to his pre-Adamic beginning, to pre-history, and this shared contagion of madness exists universally in contemporary poetry, and particularly in a poet like Samuel Beckett.

The words jerk, the search is anguished, the pronouncing of chosen nouns, the cynical or violent rejection of the named thing itself, or the primal or the final elation of the power or of the decadence of the Word itself, the process is shared by three utterly different writers, one Guyanese-African, one English-Celtic, the third Irish-Celtic. What is shared is more than the language; it is the drilling, mining, molelike or mole-cricketlike burrowing into the origins of life or into its detritus. Logos as excrement, logos as engendering spasm. In the sense that these three are black writers, we can only use the term "black" to imply a malevolence towards historical system. The Old World, or visitors to the Old World, or those who exist in the Old World, whether it is Africa, or the Yorkshire submarine world deep as England, or Beckett's unnamed, unnameable gray world of a wrecked civilization, these who are embittered by those worlds write blackly, with a purging pessimism which goes beyond the morbid. In the New World there is the same process in writers with an optimistic or visionary force, there is the same slow naming. This exists wholly in Wilson Harris. But this blackness is luminous. The black in Williams returns in his madness to beginning again. He climbs his thorn tree, he reverts to the anthropological origins of all mankind, no doubt he will descend again, and like Hughes's medieval monster undergoing his thrilling metamorphosis from demon to man as he begins to name things, and he may wreck and destroy civilization and its languages again like those crawlers through primordial and post-atomic mud in Beckett, but these three elemental cycles are the common agony of three racially different writers. These crude cycles are the poet's knowledge of history. So what does this prove? It proves that the truest writers are those who see language not as linguistic process but as a living element; it more closely demonstrates the laziness of poets who confuse language with linguistics and with archaeology. It also annihilates provincial concepts of imitation and originality. Fear of imitation obsesses minor poets. But in any age a common genius almost indistinguishably will show itself, and the perpetuity of this genius is the only valid tradition, not the tradition which categorizes poetry by epochs and by schools. We know that the great poets have no wish to be different, no time to be original, that their originality emerges only when they have absorbed all the poetry which they have read, entire, that their first work appears to be the accumulation of other people's trash, but that they become bonfires, that it is only academics and frightened poets who talk of Beckett's debt to Joyce.

The tribe requires of its poets the highest language and more than predictable sentiment. Now pardon this excursion into autobiography. I knew, from childhood, that I wanted to become a poet, and like any colonial child I was taught English literature as my natural inheritance. Forget the snow and the daffodils. They were real, more real than the heat and the oleander, perhaps, because they lived on the page, in imagination, and therefore in memory. There is a memory of imagination in literature which has nothing to do with actual experience, which is, in fact, another life, and that experience of the imagination will continue to make actual the quest of a medieval knight or the bulk of a white whale, because of the power of a shared imagination. The world of poetry was natural and unlimited by what no child really accepts as the actual world, and of course, later disenchantment and alienation will come. But these are not altogether important, they become part of maturity. To simplify: once I had decided to make the writing of poetry my life, my actual, not my imaginative life, I felt both a rejection and a fear of Europe while I learned its poetry. I have remained this way, but the emotions have changed, they are subtler, more controlled, for I would no longer wish to visit Europe as if I could repossess it than I would wish to visit Africa for that purpose. What survives in the slave is nostalgia for imperial modes, Europe or Africa. I felt, I knew, that if I went to England I would never become a poet, far more a West Indian, and that was the only thing I could see myself becoming, a West Indian poet. The language I used did not bother me. I had given it, and it was irretrievably given; I could no more give it back than they could claim it. But I fear the cathedrals, the music, the weight of history, not because I was alien, but because I felt history to be the burden of others. I was not excited by continuation of its process but by discovery, by the plain burden of work, for there was too much to do here. Yet the older and more assured I grew, the stronger my isolation as a poet, the more I needed to become omnivorous about the art and literature of Europe to understand my own world. I write "my own world" because I had no doubt that it was mine, that it was given to me, by God, not by history, with my gift. At that time nobody anatomized the honesty of my commitment, nobody urged me to reject old values, but such people would have to go through an anguish of rejection and arrogant self-assertion later. These are qualifications of faith, but they are important. We are misled by new prophets of bitterness who warn us against experiences which we have never cared to have, but the mass of society has had neither the interest nor the opportunity which they chose. These preach not to the converted but to those who have never lost faith. I do not mean religious faith but reality. Fisherman and peasant know who they are and what they are and where they are, and when we show them our wounded sensibilities we are, most of us, displaying self-inflicted wounds.

I accept this archipelago of the Americas. I say to the ancestor who sold me, and to the ancestor who bought me, I have no father, I want no such father, although I can understand you, black ghost, white ghost, when you both whisper "history," for if I attempt to forgive you both I am falling into your idea of history which justifies and explains and expiates, and it is not mine to forgive, my memory cannot summon any filial love, since your features are anonymous and erased and I have no wish and no power to pardon. You were when you acted your roles, your given, historical roles of slave seller and slave buyer, men acting as men, and also you, father in the filth-ridden gut of the slave ship, to you they were also men, acting as men, with the cruelty of men, your fellowman and tribesman not moved or hovering with hesitation about your common race any longer than my other bastard ancestor hovered with his whip, but to you, inwardly forgiven grandfathers, I, like the more honest of my race, give a strange thanks. I give the strange and bitter and yet ennobling thanks for the monumental groaning and soldering of two great worlds, like the halves of a fruit seamed by its own bitter juice, that exiled from your own Edens you have placed me in the wonder of another, and that was my inheritance and your gift.

(1974)

The Antilles:
Fragments of Epic Memory

Felicity is a village in Trinidad on the edge of the Caroni plain, the wide central plain that still grows sugar and to which indentured cane cutters were brought after emancipation, so the small population of Felicity is East Indian, and on the afternoon that I visited it with friends from America, all the faces along its road were Indian, which, as I hope to show, was a moving, beautiful thing, because this Saturday afternoon *Ramleela*, the epic dramatization of the Hindu epic the *Ramayana*, was going to be performed, and the costumed actors from the village were assembling on a field strung with different-coloured flags, like a new gas station, and beautiful Indian boys in red and black were aiming arrows haphazardly into the afternoon light. Low blue mountains on the horizon, bright grass, clouds that would gather colour before the light went. Felicity! What a gentle Anglo-Saxon name for an epical memory.

Under an open shed on the edge of the field, there were two huge armatures of bamboo that looked like immense cages. They were parts of the body of a god, his calves or thighs, which, fitted and reared, would make a gigantic effigy. This effigy would be burnt as a conclusion to the epic. The cane structures flashed a predictable parallel: Shelley's sonnet on the fallen statue of Ozymandias and his empire, that "colossal wreck" in its empty desert.

Drummers had lit a fire in the shed and they eased the skins of their tablas nearer the flames to tighten them. The saffron flames, the bright grass, and the hand-woven armatures of the fragmented god who would be burnt were not in any desert where imperial power had finally toppled but were part of a ritual, evergreen season that, like the cane-burning harvest, is annually repeated, the point of such sacrifice being its repetition, the point of the destruction being renewal through fire.

Deities were entering the field. What we generally call "Indian music" was blaring from the open platformed shed from which the epic would be narrated. Costumed actors were arriving. Princes and gods, I supposed. What an unfortunate confession! "Gods, I suppose" is the shrug that embodies our African and Asian diasporas. I had often thought of but never seen *Ramleela*, and had never seen this theatre, an open field, with village children as warriors, princes, and gods. I had no idea what the epic story was, who its hero was, what enemies he fought, yet I had recently adapted the *Odyssey* for a theatre in England, presuming that the audience knew the trials of Odysseus, hero of another Asia Minor epic, while nobody in Trinidad knew any more than I did about Rama, Kali, Shiva, Vishnu, apart from the Indians, a phrase I use pervertedly because that is the kind of remark you can still hear in Trinidad: "apart from the Indians."

It was as if, on the edge of the Central Plain, there was another plateau, a raft on which the *Ramayana* would be poorly performed in this ocean of cane, but that was my writer's view of things, and it is wrong. I was seeing the *Ramleela* at Felicity as theatre when it was faith.

Multiply that moment of self-conviction when an actor, made-up and costumed, nods to his mirror before stopping on stage in the belief that he is a reality entering an illusion and you would have what I presumed was happening to the actors of this epic. But they were not actors. They had been chosen; or they themselves had chosen their roles in this sacred story that would go on for nine afternoons over a two-hour period till the sun set. They were not amateurs but believers. There was no theatrical term to define them. They did not have to psych themselves up to play their roles. Their acting would probably be as buoyant and as natural as those bamboo arrows crisscrossing the afternoon pasture. They believed in what they were playing, in the sacredness of the text, the validity of India, while I, out of the writer's habit, searched for some sense of elegy, of loss, even of degenerative mimicry in the happy faces of the boy-warriors or the heraldic profiles of the village princes. I was polluting the afternoon with doubt and with the patronage of admiration. I misread the event through a visual echo of History—the cane fields, indenture, the evocation of vanished armies, temples, and trumpeting elephants—when all around me there was quite the opposite: elation, delight in the boys' screams, in the sweets-stalls, in more and more costumed characters appearing; a delight of conviction, not loss. The name Felicity made sense.

Consider the scale of Asia reduced to these fragments: the small white exclamations of minarets or the stone balls of temples in the cane fields, and one can understand the self-mockery and embarrassment of those who see these rites as parodic, even degenerate. These purists look on such ceremonies as grammarians look at a dialect, as cities look on provinces and empires on their colonies. Memory that yearns to join the centre, a limb remembering the body from which it has been severed, like those bamboo thighs of the god. In other words, the way that the Caribbean is still looked at, illegitimate, rootless, mongrelized. "No people there," to quote Froude, "in the true sense of the word." No people. Fragments and echoes of real people, unoriginal and broken.

The performance was like a dialect, a branch of its original language, an abridgement of it, but not a distortion or even a reduction of its epic scale. Here in Trinidad I had discovered that one of the greatest epics of the world was seasonally performed, not with that desperate resignation of preserving a culture, but with an openness of belief that was as steady as the wind bending the cane lances of the Caroni plain. We had to leave before the play began to go through the creeks of the Caroni Swamp, to catch the scarlet ibises coming home at dusk. In a performance as natural as those of the actors of the *Ramleela*, we watched the flocks come in as bright as the scarlet of the boy archers, as the red flags, and cover an islet until it turned into a flowering tree, an anchored immortelle. The sigh of History meant nothing here. These two visions, the *Ramleela* and the arrowing flocks of scarlet ibises, blent into a single gasp of gratitude. Visual surprise is natural in the Caribbean; it comes with the landscape, and faced with its beauty, the sigh of History dissolves.

We make too much of that long groan which underlines the past. I felt privileged to discover the ibises as well as the scarlet archers of Felicity.

The sigh of History rises over ruins, not over landscapes, and in the Antilles there are few ruins to sigh over, apart from the ruins of sugar estates and abandoned forts. Looking around slowly, as a camera would, taking in the low blue hills over Port of Spain, the village road and houses, the warrior-archers, the god-actors and their handlers, and music already on the sound track, I wanted to make a film that would be a long-drawn sigh over Felicity. I was filtering the afternoon with evocations of a lost India, but why "evocations"? Why not "celebrations of a real presence"? Why should India be "lost" when none of these villagers ever really knew it, and why not "continuing," why not the perpetuation of joy in Felicity and in all the other nouns of the Central Plain: Couva, Chaguanas, Charley Village? Why was I not letting my pleasure open its windows wide? I was entitled like any Trinidadian to the ecstasies of their claim, because ecstasy was the pitch of the sinuous drumming in the loudspeakers. I was entitled to the feast of Husein, to the mirrors and crêpe-paper temples of the Muslim epic, to the Chinese Dragon Dance, to the rites of that Sephardic Jewish synagogue that was once on Something Street. I am only one-eighth the writer I might have been had I contained all the fragmented languages of Trinidad.

Break a vase, and the love that reassembles the fragments is stronger than that love which took its symmetry for granted when it was whole. The glue that fits the pieces is the sealing of its original shape. It is such a love that reassembles our African and Asiatic fragments, the cracked heirlooms whose restoration shows its white scars. This gathering of broken pieces is the care and pain of the Antilles, and if the pieces are disparate, ill-fitting, they contain more pain than their original sculpture, those icons and sacred vessels taken for granted in their ancestral places. Antillean art is this restoration of our shattered histories, our shards of vocabulary, our archipelago becoming a synonym for pieces broken off from the original continent.

And this is the exact process of the making of poetry, or what should be called not its "making" but its remaking, the fragmented memory, the armature that frames the god, even the rite that surrenders it to a final pyre; the god assembled cane by cane, reed by weaving reed, line by plaited line, as the artisans of Felicity would erect his holy echo.

Poetry, which is perfection's sweat but which must seem as fresh as the raindrops on a statue's brow, combines the natural and the marmoreal; it conjugates both tenses simultaneously: the past and the present, if the past is the sculpture and the present the beads of dew or rain on the forehead of the past. There is the buried language and there is the individual vocabulary, and the process of poetry is one of excavation and of self-discovery. Tonally the individual voice is a dialect; it shapes its own accent, its own vocabulary and melody in defiance of an imperial concept of language, the language of Ozymandias, libraries and dictionaries, law courts and critics, and churches, universities, political dogma, the diction of institutions. Poetry is an island that breaks away from the main. The dialects of my archipelago seem as fresh to me as those raindrops on the statue's forehead, not the sweat made from the classic exertion of frowning marble, but the condensations of a refreshing element, rain and salt.

Deprived of their original language, the captured and indentured tribes create their own, accreting and secreting fragments of an old, an epic vocabulary, from Asia and from Africa, but to an ancestral, an ecstatic rhythm in the blood that cannot be subdued by slavery or indenture, while nouns are renamed and the given names of places accepted like Felicity village or Choiseul. The original language dissolves from the exhaustion of distance like fog trying to cross an ocean, but this process of renaming, of finding new metaphors, is the same process that the poet faces every morning of his working day, making his own tools like Crusoe, assembling nouns from necessity, from Felicity, even renaming himself. The stripped man is driven back to that self-astonishing, elemental force, his mind. That is the basis of the Antillean experience, this shipwreck of fragments, these echoes, these shards of a huge tribal vocabulary, these partially remembered customs, and they are not decayed but strong. They survived the Middle Passage and the *Fatel Rozack*, the ship that carried the first indentured Indians from the port of Madras to the cane fields of Felicity, that carried the chained

Cromwellian convict and the Sephardic Jew, the Chinese grocer and the Lebanese merchant selling cloth samples on his bicycle.

And here they are, all in a single Caribbean city, Port of Spain, the sum of history, Trollope's "non-people." A downtown babel of shop signs and streets, mongrelized, polyglot, a ferment without a history, like heaven. Because that is what such a city is, in the New World, a writer's heaven.

A culture, we all know, is made by its cities.

Another first morning home, impatient for the sunrise—a broken sleep. Darkness at five, and the drapes not worth opening; then, in the sudden light, a cream-walled, brown-roofed police station bordered with short royal palms, in the colonial style, back of it frothing trees and taller palms, a pigeon fluttering into the cover of an eave, a rain-stained block of once-modern apartments, the morning side road into the station without traffic. All part of a surprising peace. This quiet happens with every visit to a city that has deepened itself in me. The flowers and the hills are easy, affection for them predictable; it is the architecture that, for the first morning, disorients. A return from American seductions used to make the traveller feel that something was missing, something was trying to complete itself, like the stained concrete apartments. Pan left along the window and the excrescences rear—a city trying to soar, trying to be brutal, like an American city in silhouette, stamped from the same mould as Columbus or Des Moines. An assertion of power, its decor bland, its air conditioning pitched to the point where its secretarial and executive staff sport competing cardigans; the colder the offices the more important, an imitation of another climate. A longing, even an envy of feeling cold.

In serious cities, in grey, militant winter with its short afternoons, the days seem to pass by in buttoned overcoats, every building appears as a barracks with lights on in its windows, and when snow comes, one has the illusion of living in a Russian novel, in the nineteenth century, because of the literature of winter. So visitors to the Caribbean must feel that they are inhabiting a succession of postcards. Both climates are shaped by what we have read of them. For tourists, the sunshine cannot be serious. Winter adds depth and darkness to life as well as to literature, and in the unending summer of the tropics not even poverty or poetry (in the Antilles poverty is poetry with a V, *une vie*, a condition of life as well as of imagination) seems capable of being profound because the nature around it is so exultant, so resolutely ecstatic, like its music. A culture based on joy is bound to be shallow. Sadly, to sell itself, the Caribbean encourages the delights of mindlessness, of brilliant vacuity, as a place to flee not only winter but that seriousness that comes only out of culture with four seasons. So how can there be a people there, in the true sense of the word?

They know nothing about seasons in which leaves let go of the year, in which spires fade in blizzards and streets whiten, of the erasures of whole cities by fog, of reflection in fireplaces; instead, they inhabit a geography whose rhythm, like their music, is limited to two stresses: hot and wet, sun and rain, light and shadow, day and night, the limitations of an incomplete metre, and are therefore a people incapable of the subtleties of contradiction, of imaginative complexity. So be it. We cannot change contempt.

Ours are not cities in the accepted sense, but no one wants them to be. They dictate their own proportions, their own definitions in particular places and in a prose equal to that of their detractors, so that now it is not just St. James but the streets and yards that Naipaul commemorates, its lanes as short and brilliant as his sentences; not just the noise and jostle of Tunapuna but the origins of C.L.R. James's *Beyond a Boundary*, not just Felicity village

on the Caroni plain, but Selvon Country, and that is the
way it goes up the islands now: the old Dominica of Jean
Rhys still very much the way she wrote of it; and the Martinique of the early Césaire; Perse's Guadeloupe, even
without the pith helmets and the mules; and what delight
and privilege there was in watching a literature—one literature in several imperial languages, French, English,
Spanish—bud and open island after island in the early
morning of a culture, not timid, not derivative, any more
than the hard white petals of the frangipani are derivative
and timid. This is not a belligerent boast but a simple
celebration of inevitability: and this flowering had to come.

On a heat-stoned afternoon in Port of Spain, some
alley white with glare, with love vine spilling over a fence,
palms and a hazed mountain appear around a corner to
the evocation of Vaughn or Herbert's "that shady city of
palm-trees," or to the memory of a Hammond organ from
a wooden chapel in Castries, where the congregation sang
"Jerusalem, the Golden." It is hard for me to see such
emptiness as desolation. It is that patience that is the
width of Antillean life, and the secret is not to ask the
wrong thing of it, not to demand of it an ambition it has
no interest in. The traveller reads this as lethargy, as
torpor.

Here there are not enough books, one says, no theatres, no museums, simply not enough to do. Yet, deprived
of books, a man must fall back on thought, and out of
thought, if he can learn to order it, will come the urge to
record, and in extremity, if he has no means of recording, recitation, the ordering of memory which leads to
metre, to commemoration. There can be virtues in deprivation, and certainly one virtue is salvation from a cascade
of high mediocrity, since books are now not so much created as remade. Cities create a culture, and all we have
are these magnified market towns, so what are the
proportions of the ideal Caribbean city? A surrounding,

accessible countryside with leafy suburbs, and if the city is lucky, behind it, spacious plains. Behind it, fine mountains; before it, an indigo sea. Spires would pin its centre and around them would be leafy, shadowy parks. Pigeons would cross its sky in alphabetic patterns, carrying with them memories of a belief in augury, and at the heart of the city there would be horses, yes, horses, those animals last seen at the end of the nineteenth century drawing broughams and carriages with top-hatted citizens, horses that live in the present tense without elegiac echoes from their hooves, emerging from paddocks at the Queen's Park Savannah at sunrise, when mist is unthreading from the cool mountains above the roofs, and at the centre of the city seasonally there would be races, so that citizens could roar at the speed and grace of these nineteenth-century animals. Its docks, not obscured by smoke or deafened by too much machinery, and above all, it would be so racially various that the cultures of the world—the Asiatic, the Mediterranean, the European, the African—would be represented in it, its humane variety more exciting than Joyce's Dublin. Its citizens would intermarry as they chose, from instinct, not tradition, until their children find it increasingly futile to trace their genealogy. It would not have too many avenues difficult or dangerous for pedestrians, its mercantile area would be a cacophony of accents, fragments of the old language that would be silenced immediately at five o'clock, its docks resolutely vacant on Sundays.

This is Port of Spain to me, a city ideal in its commercial and human proportions, where a citizen is a walker and not a pedestrian, and this is how Athens may have been before it became a cultural echo.

The finest silhouettes of Port of Spain are idealizations of the craftsman's handiwork, not of concrete and glass, but of baroque woodwork, each fantasy looking more like an involved drawing of itself than the actual building. Behind the city is the Caroni plain, with its villages, Indian prayer flags, and fruit vendors' stalls along the highway over which ibises come like floating flags. Photogenic poverty! Postcard sadnesses! I am not re-creating Eden; I mean, by "the Antilles," the reality of light, of work, of survival. I mean a house on the side of a country road, I mean the Caribbean Sea, whose smell is the smell of refreshing possibility as well as survival. Survival is the triumph of stubbornness, and spiritual stubbornness, a sublime stupidity, is what makes the occupation of poetry endure, when there are so many things that should make it futile. Those things added together can go under one collective noun: "the world."

This is the visible poetry of the Antilles, then. Survival.

If you wish to understand that consoling pity with which the islands were regarded, look at the tinted engravings of Antillean forests, with their proper palm trees, ferns, and waterfalls. They have a civilizing decency, like Botanical Gardens, as if the sky were a glass ceiling under which a colonized vegetation is arranged for quiet walks and carriage rides. Those views are incised with a pathos that guides the engraver's tool and the topographer's pencil, and it is this pathos which, tenderly ironic, gave villages names like Felicity. A century looked at a landscape furious with vegetation in the wrong light and with the wrong eye. It is such pictures that are saddening rather than the tropics itself. These delicate engravings of sugar mills and harbours, of native women in costume, are seen as a part of History, that History which looked over the shoulder of the engraver and, later, the photographer. History can alter the eye and the moving hand to conform a view of itself; it can rename places for the nostalgia in an echo; it can temper the glare of tropical light to elegiac monotony in prose, the tone of judgement in Conrad, in the travel journals of Trollope.

These travellers carried with them the infection of

their own malaise, and their prose reduced even the landscape to melancholia and self-contempt. Every endeavor is belittled as imitation, from architecture to music. There was this conviction in Froude that since History is based on achievement, and since the history of the Antilles was so genetically corrupt, so depressing in its cycles of massacres, slavery, and indenture, a culture was inconceivable and nothing could ever be created in those ramshackle ports, those monotonously feudal sugar estates. Not only the light and salt of Antillean mountains defied this, but the demotic vigour and variety of their inhabitants. Stand close to a waterfall and you will stop hearing its roar. To be still in the nineteenth century, like horses, as Brodsky has written, may not be such a bad deal, and much of our life in the Antilles still seems to be in the rhythm of the last century, like the West Indian novel.

By writers even as refreshing as Graham Greene, the Caribbean is looked at with elegiac pathos, a prolonged sadness to which Lévi-Strauss has supplied an epigraph: *Tristes Tropiques*. Their *tristesse* derives from an attitude to the Caribbean dusk, to rain, to uncontrollable vegetation, to the provincial ambition of Caribbean cities where brutal replicas of modern architecture dwarf the small houses and streets. The mood is understandable, the melancholy as contagious as the fever of a sunset, like the gold fronds of diseased coconut palms, but there is something alien and ultimately wrong in the way such a sadness, even a morbidity, is described by English, French, or some of our exiled writers. It relates to a misunderstanding of the light and the people on whom the light falls.

These writers describe the ambitions of our unfinished cities, their unrealized, homiletic conclusion, but the Caribbean city may conclude just at that point where it is satisfied with its own scale, just as Caribbean culture is not evolving but already shaped. Its proportions are not to be measured by the traveller or the exile, but by its own citizenry and architecture. To be told you are not yet a city or a culture requires this response. I am not your city or your culture. There might be less of *Tristes Tropiques* after that.

Here, on the raft of this dais, there is the sound of the applauding surf: our landscape, our history recognized, "at last." *At Last* is one of the first Caribbean books. It was written by the Victorian traveller Charles Kingsley. It is one of the early books to admit the Antillean landscape and its figures into English literature. I have never read it but gather that its tone is benign. The Antillean archipelago was there to be written about, not to write itself, by Trollope, by Patrick Leigh-Fermor, in the very tone in which I almost wrote about the village spectacle at Felicity, as a compassionate and beguiled outsider, distancing myself from Felicity village even while I was enjoying it. What is hidden cannot be loved. The traveller cannot love, since love is stasis and travel is motion. If he returns to what he loved in a landscape and stays there, he is no longer a traveller but in stasis and concentration, the lover of that particular part of earth, a native. So many people say they "love the Caribbean," meaning that someday they plan to return for a visit but could never live there, the usual benign insult of the traveller, the tourist. These travellers, at their kindest, were devoted to the same patronage, the islands passing in profile, their vegetal luxury, their backwardness and poverty. Victorian prose dignified them. They passed by in beautiful profiles and were forgotten, like a vacation.

Alexis Saint-Léger Léger, whose writer's name is St.-John Perse, was the first Antillean to win this prize for poetry. He was born in Guadeloupe and wrote in French, but before him, there was nothing as fresh and clear in feeling as those poems of his childhood, that of a privileged white child on an Antillean plantation, *"Pour fêter une enfance,"* *"Eloges,"* and later *"Images à Crusoe."*

At last, the first breeze on the page, salt-edged and self-renewing as the trade winds, the sound of pages and palm trees turning as "the odour of coffee ascends the stairs."

Caribbean genius is condemned to contradict itself. To celebrate Perse, we might be told, is to celebrate the old plantation system, to celebrate the *bequé* or plantation rider, verandahs and mulatto servants, a white French language in a white pith helmet, to celebrate a rhetoric of patronage and hauteur; and even if Perse denied his origins, great writers often have this folly of trying to smother their source, we cannot deny him any more than we can the African Aimé Césaire. This is not accommodation, this is the ironic republic that is poetry, since, when I see cabbage palms moving their fronds at sunrise, I think they are reciting Perse.

The fragrant and privileged poetry that Perse composed to celebrate his white childhood and the recorded Indian music behind the brown young archers of Felicity, with the same cabbage palms against the same Antillean sky, pierce me equally. I feel the same poignancy of pride in the poems as in the faces. Why, given the history of the Antilles, should this be remarkable? The history of the world, by which of course we mean Europe, is a record of intertribal lacerations, of ethnic cleansings. At last, islands not written about but writing themselves! The palms and the Muslim minarets are Antillean exclamations. At last! the royal palms of Guadeloupe recite *"Eloges"* by heart.

Later, in *Anabase*, Perse assembled fragments of an imaginary epic, with the clicking teeth of frontier gates, barren wadis with the froth of poisonous lakes, horsemen burnoosed in sandstorms, the opposite of cool Caribbean mornings, yet not necessarily a contrast any more than some young brown archer at Felicity, hearing the sacred text blared across the flagged field, with its battles and elephants and monkey-gods, in a contrast to the white child in Guadeloupe assembling fragments of his own epic from the lances of the cane fields, the estate carts and oxens, and the calligraphy of bamboo leaves from the ancient languages, Hindi, Chinese, and Arabic, on the Antillean sky. From the *Ramayana* to Anabasis, from Guadeloupe to Trinidad, all that archaeology of fragments lying around, from the broken African kingdoms, from the crevasses of Canton, from Syria and Lebanon, vibrating not under the earth but in our raucous, demotic streets.

A boy with weak eyes skims a flat stone across the flat water of an Aegean inlet, and that ordinary action with the scything elbow contains the skipping lines of the *Iliad* and the *Odyssey*, and another child aims a bamboo arrow at a village festival, and another hears the rustling march of cabbage palms in a Caribbean sunrise, and from that sound, with its fragments of tribal myth, the compact expedition of Perse's epic is launched, centuries and archipelagos apart. For every poet it is always morning in the world. History a forgotten, insomniac night; History and elemental awe are always our early beginning, because the fate of poetry is to fall in love with the world, in spite of History.

There is a force of exultation, a celebration of luck, when a writer finds himself a witness to the early morning of a culture that is defining itself, branch by branch, leaf by leaf, in that self-defining dawn, which is why, especially at the edge of the sea, it is good to make a ritual of the sunrise. Then the noun, the "Antilles" ripples like brightening water, and the sounds of leaves, palm fronds, and birds are the sounds of fresh dialect, the native tongue. The personal vocabulary, the individual melody whose metre is one's biography, joins in that sound, with any luck, and the body moves like a walking, a waking island.

This is the benediction that is celebrated, a fresh language and a fresh people, and this is the frightening duty owed.

I stand here in their name, if not their image—but

also in the name of the dialect they exchange like the leaves of the trees whose names are suppler, greener, more morning-stirred than English—*laurier canelles, bois-flot, bois-canot*—or the valleys the trees mention—*Fond St. Jacques, Mabonya, Forestièr, Roseau, Mahaut*—or the empty beaches—*L'Anse Ivrogne, Case en Bas, Paradis*—all songs and histories in themselves, pronounced not in French—but in patois.

One rose hearing two languages, one of the trees, one of schoolchildren reciting in English:

> *I am monarch of all I survey,*
> *My right there is none to dispute;*
> *From the centre all round to the sea*
> *I am lord of the fowl and the brute.*
> *Oh, solitude! where are the charms*
> *That sages have seen in thy face?*
> *Better dwell in the midst of alarms,*
> *Than reign in this horrible place . . .*

While in the country to the same metre, but to organic instruments, handmade violin, chac-chac, and goatskin drum, a girl named Sensenne singing:

> *Si mwen di 'ous' ça fait mwen la peine*
> *'Ous kai dire ça vrai.*
> > *(If I told you that caused me pain*
> > *You'll say, "It's true.")*
> *Si mwen di 'ous ça pentetrait mwen*
> *'Ous peut dire ça vrai.*
> > *(If I told you you pierced my heart*
> > *You'd say, "It's true.")*
> *Ces mamailles actuellement*
> *Pas ka faire l'amour z'autres pour un rien.*
> > *(Children nowadays*
> > *Don't make love for nothing.)*

It is not that History is obliterated by this sunrise. It is there in Antillean geography, in the vegetation itself. The sea sighs with the drowned from the Middle Passage, the butchery of its aborigines, Carib and Aruac and Taino, bleeds in the scarlet of the immortelle, and even the actions of surf on sand cannot erase the African memory, or the lances of cane as a green prison where indentured Asians, the ancestors of Felicity, are still serving time.

That is what I have read around me from boyhood, from the beginnings of poetry, the grace of effort. In the hard mahogany of woodcutters: faces, resinous men, charcoal burners; in a man with a cutlass cradled across his forearm, who stands on the verge with the usual anonymous khaki dog; in the extra clothes he put on this morning, when it was cold when he rose in the thinning dark to go and make his garden in the heights—the heights, the garden, being miles away from his house, but that is where he has his land—not to mention the fishermen, the footmen on trucks, groaning up mornes, all fragments of Africa originally but shaped and hardened and rooted now in the island's life, illiterate in the way leaves are illiterate; they do not read, they are there to be read, and if they are properly read, they create their own literature.

But in our tourist brochures the Caribbean is a blue pool into which the republic dangles the extended foot of Florida as inflated rubber islands bob and drinks with umbrellas float towards her on a raft. This is how the islands from the shame of necessity sell themselves; this is the seasonal erosion of their identity, that high-pitched repetition of the same images of service that cannot distinguish one island from the other, with a future of polluted marinas, land deals negotiated by ministers, and all of this conducted to the music of Happy Hour and the rictus of a smile. What is the earthly paradise for our visitors? Two weeks without rain and a mahogany tan, and, at sunset, local troubadours in straw hats and floral shirts beating

"Yellow Bird" and "Banana Boat Song" to death. There is a territory wider than this—wider than the limits made by the map of an island—which is the illimitable sea and what it remembers.

All of the Antilles, every island, is an effort of memory; every mind, every racial biography culminating in amnesia and fog. Pieces of sunlight through the fog and sudden rainbows, *arcs-en-ciel*. That is the effort, the labour of the Antillean imagination, rebuilding its gods from bamboo frames, phrase by phrase.

Decimation from the Aruac downwards is the blasted root of Antillean history, and the benign blight that is tourism can infect all of those island nations, not gradually, but with imperceptible speed, until each rock is whitened by the guano of white-winged hotels, the arc and descent of progress.

Before it is all gone, before only a few valleys are left, pockets of an older life, before development turns every artist into an anthropologist or folklorist, there are still cherishable places, little valleys that do not echo with ideas, a simplicity of rebeginnings, not yet corrupted by the dangers of change. Not nostalgic sites but occluded sanctities as common and simple as their sunlight. Places as threatened by this prose as a headland is by the bulldozer or a sea almond grove by the surveyor's string, or from blight, the mountain laurel.

        :

One last epiphany: A basic stone church in a thick valley outside Soufrière, the hills almost shoving the houses around into a brown river, a sunlight that looks oily on the leaves, a backward place, unimportant, and one now being corrupted into significance by this prose. The idea is not to hallow or invest the place with anything, not even memory. African children in Sunday frocks come down the ordinary concrete steps into the church, banana leaves hang and glisten, a truck is parked in a yard, and old women totter towards the entrance. Here is where a real fresco should be painted, one without importance, but one with real faith, mapless, Historyless.

How quickly it could all disappear! And how it is beginning to drive us further into where we hope are impenetrable places, green secrets at the end of bad roads, headlands where the next view is not of a hotel but of some long beach without a figure and the hanging question of some fisherman's smoke at its far end. The Caribbean is not an idyll, not to its natives. They draw their working strength from it organically, like trees, like the sea almond or the spice laurel of the heights. Its peasantry and its fishermen are not there to be loved or even photographed; they are trees who sweat, and whose bark is filmed with salt, but every day on some island, rootless trees in suits are signing favourable tax breaks with entrepreneurs, poisoning the sea almond and the spice laurel of the mountains to their roots. A morning could come in which governments might ask what happened not merely to the forests and the bays but to a whole people.

They are here again, they recur, the faces, corruptible angels, smooth black skins and white eyes huge with an alarming joy, like those of the Asian children of Felicity at *Ramleela*; two different religions, two different continents, both filling the heart with the pain that is joy.

But what is joy without fear? The fear of selfishness that, here on this podium with the world paying attention not to them but to me, I should like to keep these simple joys inviolate, not because they are innocent, but because they are true. They are as true as when, in the grace of this gift, Perse heard the fragments of his own epic of Asia Minor in the rustling of cabbage palms, that inner Asia of the soul through which imagination wanders, if there is such a thing as imagination as opposed to the collective memory of our entire race, as true as the delight of that warrior-child who flew a bamboo arrow over the flags in the field at Felicity; and now as grateful a joy and a blessed fear as when a boy opened an exercise book and, within the discipline of its margins, framed stanzas that might contain the light of the hills on an island blest by obscurity, cherishing our insignificance.

(*1992*)

II /

On Robert Lowell

And we are put on earth a little space,
That we may learn to bear the beams of love . . .
—WILLIAM BLAKE

I

Biographies of poets are hard to believe. The moment they are published they become fiction, subject to the same symmetry of plot, incident, dialogue as the novel. The inarticulate wisdom of really knowing another person is not in the broad sweep of that other person's life but in its gestures; and when the biography is about a poet the duty of giving his life a plot makes the poetry a subplot. So we read from the comfort of a mould. The book becomes an extension of the armchair, the life becomes the shadow cast by the reader.

Inevitably the biographies of poets, no matter how different, become a series of ovals in frontispieces. Robert Lowell has become one of these ovals, his dates now closed, the hyphen completed.

> *We are poor passing facts,*
> *warned by that to give*
> *each figure in the photograph*
> *his living name.*

> —*"Epilogue"*

The life itself is shattering. Lowell died at sixty. Most of that life had been spent recovering from, and dreading, mental attacks, of having to say early, "My mind's not right," but more than drugs restored him. The force that is the making of poetry, while it took its toll of his mind, also saved him. His heroism is primal, his servitude to it savage. Bedlam, asylum, hospital, his bouts of mania never left him, but they also never left him mad. Clinically, they can be listed in depressing records of collapse and release, but what cannot be described in prose is their titanic bursting out of manacles.

:

All that cold sweat now congealed into an epoch, on the marble forehead of a bust! We look at the face on the book jackets, the brow shielding the eyes from the glare of pain, and we complete it as we dared not when he was alive. To use the past tense about him, not Lowell so much as "Cal," is almost unendurable. The present is the tense of his poetry. The eyes, with their look of controlled suffering, still hurt. We wince and look away.

In life we looked at that large head, heard his soft jokes, watched his circling hands, knowing that he would become one of the great dead. The jolt that we get now is reading the work as part of the past. His industry was frightening. The head was square and noble, but it was also an ordinary American head, and it was this unrelenting ordinariness that denied itself any sort of halo. He was a man of enormous pride and fanatical humility. He softened objects around him, blurred their outlines, made the everyday myopic, saw political systems as played out. History lived in his nerves, not as a subject, but as irrational repetition.

If modern suffering cannot achieve sublime tragedy but ends in breakdown, no poet before Lowell has written so close to his own nerves. The poems of his middle age recoil to the touch, raw as a fresh cut. Their progression is supposed to form a scar, exposure forcing a healing. But often, in the Notebooks, or *History*, the wound of the poem is left raw. All of his writing is about writing, all of his poetry is about the pain of making poems. The physical labour. He doesn't sweep the fragments off the floor of his study, or studio, and show you only the finished sculpture. In *History* you see the armature, the failed fragments, the revisions, the compulsions. He could have settled into a fix, but every new book was an upheaval that had his critics scuttling. They settled and watched from a distance. Then his mind heaved again, with deliberate, wide cracks in his technique. Criticism of Lowell is more seismographic than aesthetic.

His apprenticeship was a fury. In youth every phrase was compacted with the vehemence of ambition. Rhymes were wrenched to fit the hurtling metre. He could not manage an ambulatory pace. Sometimes the wheels whirred groundlessly in air; even when they gripped, the reader shared the groan of effort, the load. In *Lord Weary's Castle* couplets barrel past the senses like boxcars, too fast to read their symbols, and leave a stunned, pumping vacancy behind them.

"Time runs," he cites Marlowe, but here it lurches:

> *Time runs, the windshield runs with stars. The past*
> *Is cities from a train, until at last*
> *Its escalating and black-windowed blocks*
> *Recoil against a Gothic church. The clocks*
> *Are tolling. I am dying. The shocked stones*
> *Are falling like a ton of bricks and bones*
> *That snap and splinter and descend in glass*
> *Before a priest who mumbles through his Mass . . .*

—*"Between the Porch and the Altar"*

The detonating phrases are more than just noise, although the poem is after "the big bang," but Lowell, like any other good poet in youth, does not care for lessons in thrift. That is natural, but here the prodigality is manoeuvred, and we have, instead of excess, a strategy so forceful it repels. What sounds like passion is not heat but cold. The effects are overcalculated. Every phrase has been worked on separately to look like ease. Some layers are erased, but you can feel the vehemence of the erasures. Their basis is the pun, a brutal name for ambiguity. The windshield runs with tears as well as stars. The tears slide down the glazed iris as stars slide down the glass window of the train in the night. There is a poem in each phrase, but the pace does not match the metre. The first two lines should have had the leisure of recollection. Instead, the tears hurtle in pentameter, and the couplets increase the speed. The "at last" does not go inward, like memory, but elevates itself into address. The speed is imitated from Hart Crane, but we can see where the phrases are joined by an iron chain, whereas in Crane at his best the links are invisible:

> *How many dawns, chill from his rippling rest,*
> *The sea-gull's wings shall dip and pivot him.*

In Crane, there is one shot, one action, on which the stanza pivots, the gull's flight.

Lowell is a long distance from it:

> *We are like a lot of wild*
> *spiders crying together,*
> *but without tears . . .*
>
> —*"Fall 1961"*

not only in the casual intimacy of the lower-case beginning (it was he who made me drop capitals from my lines), but also in the technical poignancy of this other train poem, the slackened-tic assurance of "The Mouth of the Hudson."

> *A single man stands like a bird-watcher,*
> *and scuffles the pepper and salt snow*
> *from a discarded, gray*
> *Westinghouse Electric cable drum.*
> *He cannot discover America by counting*
> *the chains of condemned freight-trains*
> *from thirty states. They jolt and jar*
> *and junk in the siding below him.*

In the earlier poem, from *Lord Weary's Castle*, the train, like time, is racing. In the later poem, the cars of the freight train are clanking and trundling to a halt.

> *His eyes drop,*
> *and he drifts with the wild ice*
> *ticking seaward down the Hudson,*
> *like the blank sides of a jig-saw puzzle.*

The years that brought this difference, this reconciliation with ambition, lie in the prose word "ticking." It is the sound of cracking ice, of a bomb, of wheels, of a clock, of the floe, fated to melt as it gets near the ocean, and every word around it is ordinary. That is, it is ordinary at first, then it is wonderful.

By the time he did his translation of the *Oresteia*, an achievement in modern dramatic verse which critics have ignored, Lowell understood technical serenity. He had blent Williams with Aeschylus. He saw the light on the brick opposite his apartment in New York not as the radiance in Shelley, or the marble light of Yeats, or the ineffable light of Wordsworth, but as light in New York, on modern brick.

:

Style sits easily on good poets, even in conversation. In intimacy, their perceptions go by so rapidly that a few drinks with them are worth a book on poetics.

In his apartment, about to go out somewhere with him, I fix the knot of Cal's tie. He returns the knot to its loose tilt. "Casual elegance," he says, his hands too large to be those of a boulevardier. The correction was technical, one moment's revelation of style. His verse, in that period of two close books, *Near the Ocean* and *For the Union Dead*, had the casual symmetry of a jacket draped on a chair, genius in shirtsleeves. He has written about the stiffness that had paralyzed his metre, how he found its rigidities unbearable to recite, skipping words when he read in public to contract them like asides. He had learned this from Beat poetry and William Carlos Williams. Still, his free verse was not a tieless metre. Debt to ancestry, to the poets who had been his masters, went too deep for that. The "Fords in search of a tradition" could dress in the striped vests of "new money," he would wear his metre loosely with ancestral hauteur.

On another occasion, and the reader must not think that I have a fetish about poets' ties, I admired, with casualness, a pale orange-and-brown-figured tie he wore. He took it off and gave it to me. I did not fawn on Lowell the poet. I did not collect bits of his clothing like his valet. Yet he once made a terrible accusation as if I were. "You use people," he told me. It was a night when he was "going off." Darkness hadn't yet come, but the light was dimming. I didn't know, as his older friends knew, how to recognize the spark that meant that, like Hieronymo, he would be mad again.

The insult went deep. Did he think that I had cultivated his friendship to advance my career? I was not an

American poet. I did not think in those terms. For there to be a career there has to be a tradition, and my new literature had none. A career, like that of any explorer's, was instantaneous. Did I feed off his verse like a parasite to fatten my own? *That* I would have confessed to, because his influence was irresistible, yet what imagination was more omnivorous than his? Yes, I said to myself, above the pain, I had used him. But only as I had used other masters, ancient or modern.

In mania veritas. Sing to me, Muse, the mania of Achilles, not the "rage," he had written, updating Homer. I had never confronted the grotesque Lowell, who struck the terror of pity in those who loved him. If Cal was drowning in the darkness at the back of his mind, it was still an illumination.

My style had been, perhaps still is, that of the magpie. A bit here, a bit there, hopping from one poet to another, but it wasn't that of the buzzard. I had practised Imitations all my life, and I had given up hope of not sounding like Lowell. At Stanley Kunitz's apartment in the Village one afternoon, Anthony Hecht, Stanley, Lowell, Henry Rago, who was then editor of *Poetry*, and I had been reading. We had not come there to read, but Cal liked reading among friends. I had a poem called "A Letter to Brooklyn." Rago said, "It's like a female Lowell." This was a little new. Talk of a cleaning maid would have been better, but too many American writers did not know the art of the insult. They undertook epigrams and it came out gossip.

:

I've described the sundering that put me off Lowell for a long time—during which he went into a hospital and I cursed and told everyone, yes, I too was tired of his turmoil. But I want to record, tears edging my eyes when he invited me years later to his apartment on West Sixty-seventh Street, the dissolving sweetness of reconciliation. He opened the door, hunched, gentle, soft-voiced, while he muttered his apology, I gave him a hard hug, and the old love deepened. The eyes were still restless, haunted. A phantom paced behind the fanlight of the irises. He reached into the inside pocket of his jacket. I knew why. For a snapshot of his daughter and my son, who are the same age, that had been taken at a beach house in Trinidad.

During the breach I had asked his friends how badly he had treated them. Violently. Unutterably. Forgivably. I never heard any stories. I did not probe. Their shock, the trauma of awful memory protected him. "Pity the monsters," he had written.

We think of the sanity of John Clare, a brightness between demonic clouds, of Poe staggering through hell in Baltimore, of Crane's or Berryman's drunkenness, but the clear and ordinary Lowell—he could recover rapidly —often showed no scar of the recent agony. The mania of elation is a kind of despair, but what biographer could catch the heartbreaking smile, his wit, his solicitude, his shyness?

:

It is this that has made things so difficult for his biographers. They settle for the easier thing, plot the manic bouts, the devastating attacks, and the agonized recovery. It is the old nineteenth-century diagnosis of the poet as madman. And how easy it is to fit Lowell into that tradition, some would say the natural inheritance of damned genius, of which Poe is the high priest. Lowell was not a madman or a *poète maudit*; he was a great poet who had devastating bouts of mental illness. Clouds covered him, but when they went, he was extraordinarily gentle. He had that masculine sweetness that draws a deep love from men.

It is its unrelenting fierceness that makes one want to ask of the poetry, as one did of the man, why it drives itself so hard. Why can't it forgive itself? The answer is that Lowell did not lie. There was no Byzantium for him, as there was for Yeats, a gold-hammered and artificial paradise which became true because need had created faith. There was no white rose in which all substances cohere at the end, as for Dante. Once, I asked him what he thought of Hopkins's "Wreck of the Deutschland." He smiled: "All those nuns." He had written in his youth about nuns, demented, passion-starved, but faith had gone. He could have mourned the loss of faith with a ripened, elegiac softness, with melody. But he had no heaven left. He had no symbol to seal his torment, like Yeats's singing mechanical bird or the rose of Eliot. American heraldry provided only "the sharp-shinned hawk in the birdbook there."

What this says about the whole quivering body of Lowell's poetry, strapped down, drugged, or domestically blissful, is what has to be said about poetry written in English from Caedmon to this minute. No other poetry I can think of is as tender, as vulnerable, in which a pitiless intelligence records its own suffering. The closest parallel is Meredith's *Modern Love*. "To live a life," Pasternak wrote, "is not to cross a field." Lowell refuses to let go of himself. It is not masochistic, this refusal, but a process of watching how poetry works, to learn if it can heal; and if poetry is a beak that plucks at the liver, like Villon, or Prometheus, then Prometheus becomes Aeschylus, the victim is his own subject, the vulture becomes a companion. He never took time "off" as a poet, like some American writers who like to say that they do other things apart from writing: farm, fish.

> No help from his body, the whale's
> warm-hearted blubber, foundering down
> leagues of ocean, gasping whiteness.
> The barbed hooks fester. The lines snap tight.

—"The Drinker"

"We asked to be obsessed with writing, and we were," he writes.

Once, I told him how much I admired that line of his in which the ice floes are compared to the blank sides of a jigsaw puzzle, and asked him how long it took him to see that. He said, "It was like pulling teeth." But a line from the same poem, "Westinghouse Electric cable drum," he had gotten from his daughter, who had been skipping along repeating it. It was Harriet, too, who had given him the line "We are like a lot of wild spiders crying together, but without tears."

　：

A writer worries and works away from his fate, and he becomes it. Lowell has joined the "long-haired sages breezing through the Universe," the transcendentalists, Emerson, Hawthorne. The New England sanity, married to the Southern, the gothic; the sounds of the sane Atlantic wind in the Southern cypress are blended in the soft, prose lilt of the later poetry, the triple adjectives that became a signature of Lowell's and of his second wife, Elizabeth Hardwick. But he has also joined those sepia ovals of New England. In his youth they drove him south in search of a more fragrant soil, a more calming fragrance than rank salt, but their magnet pulled him back to his ancestry in the Notebooks and *History*. He judged the politics of the world in the only way he could, with a puritanical harshness as fierce as his ancestors'.

Poetry is not the redemption of conduct. Anyone standing on the opposite side of this commemoration of mine, without knowing Lowell, could contradict it from the cruel litany that biography must provide. The row at the writer's colony at Yaddo, where he hounded a woman for what he thought were her Communist politics, is horribly degrading; the shambles of his marriages are a feminist's battlefield: the first, to Jean Stafford, full of drunken

violence. Nor does a penitential or remorseful poem absolve the past by its music. But we have all done awful
things, and most biographies that show the frightening
side of their subjects have a way of turning us into moral
hypocrites. Lowell, in his ranting mania, a full Caligula,
when, to use a West Indian phrase, "the power had gone
to his head," fantasized dictatorship. To me these fantasies
are not merely paranoia but a way of absorbing universal
guilt, as a child comforts himself by becoming the demon
that he imagines in the dark. When Lowell's sanity broke,
the evils of our century flooded his brain with horrors.
Original sin or the political ingenuousness of democracy
were not enough. The tortured blended with their torturer,
and his brain was one arena for both. Besides, his delu-
sions were both demonic and angelic. Like Faust, he could
mutter, "I myself am hell," but he turned one aspect of
paranoia into serenity with *Imitations*, making honey from
the bile of his illness.

In taking on the voices of poets he loved and
unashamedly envied, he could, in rewriting them, inhabit
each statue down the pantheon of the dead and move his
hand in theirs. It was high fun. But it is also benign possession. He did it with living poets, too: Montale, Unga-
retti. He becomes Sappho, Rilke, Pasternak, and writes
some of his finest poetry through them, particularly
Rilke. His imitation of "Orpheus and Eurydice," to me, is
more electric than its original. This shocks scholars. They
think that Lowell thought himself superior to these poets.
He was only doing what was a convention for the Eliza-
bethans, often improving certain lines by imitation,
heightening his own gift. The ambition that saw itself as
Milton when he wrote "The Quaker Graveyard in Nan-
tucket" and the derangement that once believed it was the
author of "Lycidas" both gave us the sunlit sanity of his
"Imitations." Some of them, for me, fail: Rimbaud seems

too sanitized; the Villon ballade, thanks to Williams, too flat for a remorseful echo. Still, he had the honesty to know his greatness, to make the great his colleagues.

:

"I have known three great poets," Auden said, "and each one was a prime son-of-a-bitch." In *History*, Lowell says this of himself. There are no secret passages. Many of them open, fetid with remorse. Like Meredith, Lowell is a poet of modern marriage. In *Modern Love*, as in "To Speak of Woe That Is in Marriage" from *Life Studies* and in much of the Notebooks, a flat, frightening chill comes off the lines, like the look of a kitchen knife. Knife, or legendary sword dividing lovers, "deep questioning," it "probes to endless dole" (*Modern Love*). And there is much that is Victorian in Lowell: divorce as death, guilt, the lines used to lash the mind to penitence. Meredith used the word "modern" with moral sarcasm. Lowell's orals aren't modern. The guilt of his adulteries, even if he thought his heart had gone cold and was only ashes, was still seen by the dance of hellfire; the woe that is in marriage was not merely modern neurosis as anatomized by Updike but a burning pit.

Without faith, without a belief in absolution and therefore of forgiveness, yet also without the remorseful terror of damnation, he talks through the grille of his lines like a confessional, a poet confessing not to religion but to poetry, the life of errors that he has committed for its sake. "My eyes have seen what my hand did." Unlike Villon, he had lost the Virgin.

Disturbing as they are in their domestic intimacies, the moral of the Notebooks is forgiveness. Lowell preempted the task of his biographers. The poems are there not to justify conduct or excuse the brutalities of betrayal but to make whatever would be said of him and those whom he had hurt audible and open to accusation, even disgust and censure while he lived. In this he went even further than Meredith, or Hardy, whom he admired. What his biographers would have revealed about him, in his collected letters, his official "life" as a postmortem, was made as open as a collection of his posthumous papers.

In some ways the Notebooks are like an index to Dante. We are in a dark wood. But the light at the end of the tunnel, as he wrote, is an oncoming train, and there is no paradise but domestic bliss.

II

All autumn, the chafe and jar
of nuclear war;
we have talked our extinction to death.

—"Fall 1961"

In the large, squat glasses of golden whiskey, of smoky bourbon, the ice kept tinkling like literary gossip. If there were two or three too many in their apartment on Sixty-seventh Street, I felt like an intruding shadow when the Lowells had guests. The couches and the books in their high bookcases, the highest of which had to be reached by a sliding ladder, were comforting, but not the portrait of some ancestor on the wall, a face with a frogged, pert authority that looked like the British Prime Minister Hugh Gaitskell. I remember something vague and golden about this ancestor and his horse, but the lineage did not interest me. Nor, for that matter, the friendly malice with which the work of colleagues was dismissed by the guests. Whole reputations crunched out like butts. It was just New York, but with others there, it was a casual salon. It was inescapably a salon, since Elizabeth Hardwick and Robert Lowell, a brilliant prose writer and the best poet in America, were married. It was midtown Manhattan, but it was also a fact of literary history, like the Brownings or the

Carlyles. This is not meant as a violation of intimacy. It is as much a setting for some of the poems in *Life Studies* and *History*.

This was when he looked happiest, I thought, in those dusks at the apartment. Also, this was the end of a day of hard work, hours on hours put in in his study, one flight up. Lowell went to work like an artisan, putting in a full day on his lines. Like all great poets he believed not in "inspiration" but in labour. We know his working methods. They brought on cold sweats, but at the end of the day, usually, exhaustion had him a little high, and the golden, iced drinks had been earned.

I cherish those visits. They are ticking ice and amber. They have the casual and comforting depth of sofas, with Cal's voice as soft as a fire, Elizabeth's curly golden hair and her high, rocking screech, and her habit of reaching out to pat your hands with a smile. "Honey," she'd smile, with a voice as sweet and slow as that substance, and they were honeyed evenings all right. The Lowells made me feel comfortable in New York. Then things darkened. We lost touch, as they say, and then he was in England.

:

In the darker passages of the Notebooks, a low ground mist, like English weather, came off the lines and obscured the figure of Lowell. He does not break clear of it, or wait for weather to lift, for the clouds that scud across the page to pass and the white to re-emerge. It is not willfulness. The syntax of the Notebooks, its disconnectedness, asides, may look perverse, and with each new line we hope for the light to break. We would like the figure of the poet to step closer, to stand still in a pool or shaft of revelation. In poets who know, either in themselves or by their fame, that they have become great, that, for whatever it means, they have achieved immortality alive, we can sense the marble hardening in their poems, the casual mannerism of every gesture immobilizing itself. A lazy or calculating Lowell could have earned that soundless applause readers give a famous poet's emblematic postures. Yeats, cloaked, striding in the great storm that is in his mind (applause), the canonical Eliot (applause), Frost in his freckled light in the fall woods (applause). The Notebooks, instead, refuse to become heraldic, they keep refusing to be poetry.

Turner and Whistler did the same thing in painting, refusing the summary of the canvas as an idea, scumbling, chafing the strokes till the solidity and known outlines of its subjects blended into the coarseness of the surface. Lowell would love to have been Constable or Vermeer. I asked him what painter he imagined to be his complement, and he said Vermeer. But in his late work, the light comes not from one but from all directions, and it is dim and shifting. We squint through the thicket.

It is important to try to assess this work not as confession or psychology, not even as poetry that proves the chaos of his life or our own, but as technique. Poets take on enormous challenges of technique, first of all in fun. His friend Berryman's "Dream Songs" prompted that competition, the way athletes challenge one another without envy. Once caught in this race, he could not stop. Berryman had devised a stanza form that was just right for his snarls of self-abuse, his alcoholic asides, self-insults, elations. Shambling, shaggy, yelping or muttering, the stanzas have the jagged shape of a manic graph. Lowell heard his mind talk and directed it gently, but without bending it into a formal structure of rhyme or the conclusive homilies of a couplet. He simply lopped it off when he knew its length was right. It is the instinct of the stonemason, the instinct that knows the weight and fit of each block, rough-edged, and fitting into a structure whose ultimate shape is unclear, not drawn in advance. The style is gothic.

It keeps going till it becomes cathedral, tapestry. Only death stops it. His last book, *Day by Day*, is filled with this exhaustion, after *History*.

:

Lowell wrote little prose, few critical essays. He did some reviewing, short pieces, and there is "Revere Street" in *Life Studies*, in which the poems themselves break from prose. Compared to Graves, Pound, Williams, Eliot, Yeats, he did not buttress his poetry with polemics, with the politics of his literary platform. Eliot fortified his direction with essays that supported his campaign; his essays were as much warnings about a change in style as they were self-endorsements. Pound, who was hardly ever wrong about poetry, wrote like a defrocked professor. For Lowell, living in America, prose must have seemed like another aspect of show business. It is the one form that is really respected because it is accessible, democratic, a thing everyone can be invited to share. It can drive the poet who only wants to use words in verse, not in explication, into loneliness or to arrogance.

This is putting it too simply, of course, but it accounts for that sense of public responsibility which American poetry has, its manic alternatives of an isolated madness or the common sense of day by day. It divides American poetry as surely as it divided Lowell's psyche, into the sane (not the Apollonian, just plain American common sense) and the crazy (not the Dionysian, just the disturbed, the misfit). On the one side are the sane poets like Williams, Bishop, Frost, Stevens (a didactic aesthete), on the other, Crane, Poe, Weldon Kees, Berryman. Lowell did not veer maniacally between those states. He did not fear wildness as did his good friend Randall Jarrell, who kept his verse as sane as his criticism; he was not as wild as Roethke or Berryman. The wildness, wrestled into a taut hysteria, tight-lipped control, took its toll of Plath, Sexton: it led to "confessional" poetry, to the compulsion to conform.

Ginsberg, to save himself from derangement, loosened all the valves, and his scream, *Howl*, gushes like scalding steam.

Instead, Lowell had a sense of structure, of technical order that was so strong it saved his mind and his work. It could look down on himself as a subject. To have destroyed himself would have been to interrupt his work. He made his madness a subject. The moral strength of this is astonishing. Waves wash and batter him, and he never falls overboard. Even when he ditched orthodoxy he had faith. In poetry. This was the New Englander in him.

:

The last time I saw him he was elated but tired. He had just published *Day by Day*. *Day by Day* is really the Notebooks truncated. The exhalations, the short, tired intakes of his last lines are a commentary on the labour, the turmoil of the preceding books. It peers at the light, no longer interested in great subjects.

History, the title with which he renamed the Notebooks, had been attacked by Geoffrey Grigson for having everything thrown in. That was the point. The poet who never relented in his undertaking to be, even in private, the conscience of America, of the twentieth-century mind, did not, could not, repeat the collage of beached fragments that is *The Waste Land*. The shards, rubble, waste were not the subject of the poem but in the mind of the poet itself. The metre of the poem has potholes, the step is irregular. It rushes, rests, gets up again, labours on. It follows Donne's injunction that the poem itself reproduce the action of its journey, and "about it and about must go."

Once we are used to heraldic, anthologized poems, we demand of poetry something more than merely loving it. We rummage in the unread, difficult, even failed poems of those whose great labours have grown dust. The real Browning, the real Donne, the real Ben Jonson are not in their lyrics but in their verse-letters, book-long monodramas, elegies, and speeches in dead plays. *Notebook*, as I wrote to Lowell when I read Grigson's jeer, will remain a mine for hardworking poets. Jaded sometimes by the music of poetry, we look for something else, something hard, complex, embedded: the ore itself. It was this search that turned Keats inward away from sweetness and bombast and that Lowell pursued further and further in each new book. Those who were irritated that he did not stick to a known path, his own path, however brambled and thick, but had turned off again into something even more complicated and lonely, were angry that he seemed to want to get lost. The poems can be infuriating, they are simply "too hard." But if one, as their reader, learns how to listen, they are, for technique, masterful. And is this not the quality that Lowell brought to twentieth-century verse, the gift required from the reader of not just reciting along with the poet, be it Hart Crane, or Stevens, or Williams, but of listening? The utter refining of the ear, the supreme compliment to our intelligence?

Lowell blessed others before he blessed himself. The benediction, wild as this sounds, is like Blake's. Everything is holy, but everything suffers. Light itself is a burden.

    :

In Trinidad, in a stone house by the sea at night, a place where we spent vacations, we lit pressure lamps because there was no electricity. The house was on a small cliff above the white noise of the Atlantic, and once the salty darkness had set in and the trees went into the night, the hiss of the gas lanterns was like a far surf. The light from the hung lanterns made a wide ring of huge shadows, dividing our faces sharply into bright and dark, like old paintings. The night air was salt, damp, and full of the steady noise of the sea; and when I think of my family there, our cook, Lizzie and Harriet, my son Peter and my wife Margaret, it is always by the light of a phrase in Pas-

ternak's poem about women sewing. "Two women, by a
Svetlan lamp's reflection / among its heavy burdens beam
and gleam." In such windy places the light made by fuel
lamps is both a burden and a benediction.

We had invited the Lowells to spend a weekend there
with us. They were going to Brazil. Lowell had just published *Imitations*. When I think of his book I think of
the sea, the night, the gas lamp, my family then, near the
ocean. He showed me the poems and asked me my opin-
ion of them. The honour I felt before his humility remains.
He did this with many people. I admired his adaptation
of Rilke's poem "Homecomings"—"The terrible Egyptian
mater-familias" sitting like Madame Récamier on her tomb
lid, the substitution of a sarcophagus for a sofa, and the
daring phrase "her breasts spread apart like ox-horns."
"Are these Rilke?" I asked him. "No," he said, "two stanzas
in there are mine." He looked pleased by my question.

To purists or scholars the "Imitations" were inso-
lence, violation, pride. But after *Imitations* Lowell had
reached a happiness in his work in which all poetry was
his. He had made the body of literature his body, all styles
his style, every varying voice his own. The "Imitations"
were not appropriations but simply a rereading of literature in his own soft accent. I remember him watching me
in the half-darkness, in one of the used-up armchairs of
the beach house. I remember feeling that he had given me
them to read not for my admiration but for a pleasure as
soft, as dim, as companionable as the darkness.

:

I was at the Chelsea Hotel in September 1977 when a
friend called to say that Cal had died. I felt more irritation
than shock. Death felt like an interruption, an impudence.
The voice was immortal in the poems and others after me
would hear it. In his last book, *Day by Day*, he had made
exhaustion inspiration. He had married often, but his
muse was not widowed. He had been faithful to her in

sickness and in health that was generally convalescence.
To the last he refused to be embalmed by fame:

> Those blessed structures, plot and rhyme—
> why are they no help to me now
> I want to make
> Something imagined, not recalled?
> . . .
> All's misalliance.
> Yet why not say what happened?
> Pray for the grace of accuracy
> Vermeer gave to the sun's illumination . . .

—"Epilogue"

(1984)

On Hemingway

The light in the Virgin Islands is almost temperate and the islands' flatness intensifies the glare. Their hills are not as lush as the islands to the south, and there is a Dutch sanity to their architecture that has nothing of the ramshackle adventurousness of the Catholic islands. Such differences are as imperceptible to the tourist as distinctions between the shires of England or the New England states. But the difference for me may have been more political than anything else. After all, they were American territory and their history was as recent and simple as American history. The low bare landscapes and white houses guarded by wispy trees, the marshes and the brightness of the coral-bottomed water were the climate of the Gulf Stream, were the territory of Hemingway.

"The water of the Stream was usually a dark blue when you looked at it when there was no wind. But when you walked out into it there was just the green light of the water over that floury white sand and you could see the shadow of any big fish a long time before he could ever come in close to the beach."

The painter evoked is Winslow Homer in the Bahamas. His hero Thomas Hudson's subjects are those of Homer in the Caribbean: waterspouts, natives fishing, storms, and beaches. The fictional painter's and his model's work are not similar just because they share a geography, they are identical in style. The style is realism based on an intimate experience of weather, essential observation that achieves authority. Hemingway does not describe Hudson's method of painting Caribbean light and nature; we know nothing about his palette or his technique except for the author's endorsement that he knows how to paint these things well enough to make them real and earn him security.

The prose itself, each paragraph framed like a series of watercolours, is Thomas Hudson's painting. Authority, selection of detail, and, above all, transparency are achieved without murk. We look through the prose itself like light and are informed about Hudson's style by the way in which the prose depicts its subject.

The subjects Thomas Hudson selects are the same as Winslow Homer's. "Tom, I want you to be a *big* partner," Bobby said, "leave all that chicken stuff behind. You've just been wasting yourself . . . Painting a Negro turning a loggerhead turtle on the beach . . ."

(See Homer's *Turtle Pound*)

. . . "Or painting two Negroes in a dinghy bullying a mess of crawfish."

Hudson turns down his friend Bobby's vision of the Last Judgement in the tropics.

"There was a man named Bosch could paint very well along these lines."

Just as, later, Hemingway turns down the inclination to depict the hell of tropical degradation and disease. And the reasons are several. Exhaustion, modesty, helplessness, the surrender of ambition. The modesty is Hemingway's confession that he dare not try depicting these things anymore, that all he believes in is what he has learnt to do well, not as a great, but as a good writer.

Homer was no innovator of technique unless one wishes to call naturalism invention, and today many of his large oils look too literary, too rhetorical, too set up, despite their accuracies. What was considered raw and powerful is sometimes reduced by its narrative element, as in *The Lifeline* or *The Lifeboat* or *The Gulfstream*, to theatricality. In the famous painting of the Negro on the cabin of a broken-masted boat, everything is in, circling sharks, and a storm gathering above the waterspouts on the horizon. It is authority that carries it beyond mere illustration, the authority which carries naturalist painting beyond the studio to equal, in light and texture, the life from which it is drawn.

It is the same authority which carries *Islands in the Stream* beyond the study or studio, beyond the Victorian picaresque and the movie melodrama, to the real Caribbean light from which it is made. The melodramatics in both Homer and Hemingway are dismissible because nature is the subject, not what is enacted in it, but the nature that surrounds and engulfs the action. In *To Have and Have Not*, in *The Old Man and the Sea*, and in *Islands in the Stream*, the Gulf Stream is the killer.

The same beautifully painted and beautifully written Gulf Stream which Homer and Hemingway could show so benignly carries Harry Morgan, the modern pirate, to nothing, like the "nigger" on the broken boat in Homer's painting; it carries the Old Man "too far out," and in one of its brackish inlets Thomas Hudson is fatally shot.

But Hemingway, like Homer, never exaggerates nature, he is always astonishingly exact. A writer has to have the light itself in his wrist to produce such clarity, to have brought out for us in the islands, by the same masterly strokes that every Caribbean watercolourist must admire in Winslow Homer, such an exhilarating "rightness."

In the Caribbean weather it is not a mood of fiction or of the tone of a painting. It is the way of life, and that life, like Anselmo's in *The Old Man and the Sea*, is a life of privation and suffering in brilliant scenery. The sea is beautiful, and it starves or feeds, and one has to learn its omens and promises; the hungry have to read all its signals, subtler because the light has no seasons: the difference between Hudson's love of the Gulf Stream and Anselmo's is the difference between America and the Caribbean, between, say, pre-Castro Harry Morgan and Thomas Hudson.

"F—— his revolution!" is Harry Morgan's slogan to the Cuban patriot. In *Islands in the Stream* Thomas Hudson, passing the slums in his chauffeur-driven car, meditates:

This was the part he did not like on the road into town. This was really the part he carried the drink for. I drink against poverty, dirty, four-hundred-year-old dust, the nose-snot of children, cracked palm fronds, roofs made from hammered tins, the shuffle of untreated syphilis, sewage in the old beds of brooks, lice on the bare necks of infested poultry, scale on the backs of old men's necks, the smell of old women, and the full-blast radio, he thought. It is a hell of a thing to do. I ought to look at it closely and do something about it. Instead you have your drink the way they carried smelling salts in the old days.

The passage is defeat without anger. Between Harry Morgan's anarchy and Thomas Hudson's withdrawal lies the corpse of Robert Jordan, who sacrifices his life, who has looked at it closely and done something about it for the poor of Spain in *For Whom the Bell Tolls*, and the corpse is Hemingway himself.

This is sad, of course, but it is honest futility, a confession of spiritual exhaustion not of contempt, inertia more real than the heroics of the preceding books. Its numbed nerve centre is despair.

Thomas Hudson does not paint that catalogue of degradation and disease any more than Winslow Homer would have. He paints an elegiac Eden, not a paradise of escape but one of healing. He is not a great but a "good" painter. The difference between Thomas Hudson and Robert Jordan is the difference between Winslow Homer and Goya, between the Spain of *For Whom the Bell Tolls* and Spanish Cuba. All around Hudson a revolution is beginning, but cynicism and too many wounds have made him numb. His refuge is drink, and although as usual with Hemingway's heroes he can down a staggering number of drinks and remain eloquent and lucid, the dependency on alcohol is more clinical than in any of the previous books in which booze is both initiation and talisman. Among other things, *Islands in the Stream* is a desperate book, an alcoholic's confession of loneliness, fear, failed marriages, boredom, and resignation to having a "good," not a great, talent.

After that, whatever the objection, we have to understand how confessional, in fact penitential, is *Islands in the Stream*. It is Hemingway's most conservative yet most confessional book. It is as conservative, as non-innovative, as Winslow Homer's painting is from our viewpoint in time. Hudson is a conservative painter. Conservative in both senses in that not only is his technique traditional but also, by recording the nature which he loves as well as he can, he is also conserving it. And this is one of the strongest currents in Hemingway's Caribbean fiction, as strong as it was in "Big Two-Hearted River" or in "Miró's Spain," that we are destroying the beauty of the earth. Thomas Hudson goes to the Gulf Stream, and the still unspoilt nature of its banks, like a convert to a font after war, divorce, drink, and despair.

In this way Hemingway is a West Indian writer, because wounded as he was, he found this part of America new, as new as Twain found the Mississippi. So was the Gulf Stream to him, but that mystery goes deeper in *Islands in the Stream* than it does in the oversymbolized parable of *The Old Man and the Sea*. Thomas Hudson is no folklore Christ or New World Ulysses but a banal and vulnerable man.

He is a privileged man, of course, but like every artist his privileges are wounds. We don't see much social conscience, but what we see is truer: personal remorse, loneliness, a mutilated humility, failure with happiness, and, truest of all, confessed selfishness. So Thomas Hudson and Hemingway record the brilliance and beauty of the northern Caribbean as men badly wounded by life, to the point of futility, so deeply that the pain is beyond concern for the spectacle of poverty and deprivation around them! They have fought for it. They have seen it all over the world. Except for its racy, melodramatic finale, *Islands in the Stream* is an honest and sad book, and it is piercingly touching in the homage it renders to the beauty of the Caribbean. It sanctifies the climate it describes. Boring in many stretches, garrulous, egomaniacal, it is as true and ordinary as life, the life it offers up in the end as a sacrifice is offered in gratitude to an Eden.

And yet, despite the admiration, there is something which the Caribbean writer holds in reserve: that the Caribbean of Hemingway is too often the old idea of the Great Outdoors, like the harbours of the Bahamas and the Virgin Islands, the Tourist, the Charter-Boat Adventure. It is, in *To Have and Have Not*, considerably there, it is beatified in *The Old Man and the Sea*, and it is penitentially or callously there in much of *Islands in the Stream*.

A disorientation is taking place which lessens a great deal of literature. Because the native, the exotic, the victim, the noble savage is looking back, returning a stare, while using a language whose definitions, whose very nouns can be reversible, it is only the absolute master-pieces of compassion that will survive. On that scale there are few great writers; only those whose authority is universal remain invaluable. History will consign the rest to its ironies.

This does not mean that a new literature from the Third World will correct and redeem the false master-pieces of the Old; in fact, writing, or art as a whole, that sets out with the purpose of rewriting literature in black or brown would be choosing an even more provincial role than that of being the exotic native. A vaster, total, race-less compassion is required of the modern writer. The divisions are sharper, the contrasts more dramatic, the hierarchy of hero, servant, and savage or exotic hordes, a hierarchy which is still the social basis of *Islands in the Stream*, is being dismantled; in fact, it is finished, and it is only in the outpost resorts of the New American empire that it survives, if not as reality, at least as romance.

The seaside bars from the Bahamas to Tobago are full of boiled executives downing drinks and looking out with unshaven machismo to the lather-line of the reefs, their scuba gear conspicuously heaped like infantry weapons. They grunt about groupers and fire coral, as if Hemingway weren't dead and all the sharks and stingrays that never attack the natives hadn't gone with him.

But something more happens in Hemingway, and it supersedes all his vanity. What happens is the opposite, a humility that he never lost towards the art of writing. That humility is in the service of the natural world and not that of the bars, the boasting, and the violence.

"You know how it is in the morning . . ." is the first paragraph in *To Have and Have Not*, and you not only know how it is, it resembles what he wrote if you have gotten up before the sun comes over the hill-roofs of Christiansted, and the light then begins to paint the closed shacks and the harbour with its white yachts and the reef line beyond the harbour make you believe that you are walking in the same light that comes off his prose.

(*1990*)

C.L.R. James

George John, Arthur Jones, Josh Rudder, Piggott, Wilton St. Hill, Matthew Boardman—the roll is like a chronicle of fallen yeomen in a Shakespearean battle, but they were cricketers of African descent who brought glory to an English game in the West Indies. Their battlefields were ringed with quietly clapping spectators. Most fell victim to prejudice and neglect. They have found a grateful chronicler in C.L.R. James, whose book *Beyond a Boundary* (published in England in 1963 but not here until 1984) should find its place on the team with Izaak Walton, Ivan Turgenev, A. J. Liebling, and Ernest Hemingway, unless its author suffers the same fate as his black subjects. *Beyond a Boundary* is a book about grace, about slow-bowlers with the wrists of anglers and fast-bowlers with the thunder of fighting bulls, and every one of its sentences, deftly turned, is like a lesson in that game, whose criterion is elegance. Mr. James can make a late-cut (a stroke in which the batsman slices the ball to the boundary as late as possible) with a phrase with the casual power of any of his heroes, from the spade-bearded W. G. Grace to willowy Garfield Sobers, but this book goes further afield than cricket. It goes behind the rusted tin forces of the barrack yards of West Indian life as far as the Periclean archipelago. And the Greek past is a lesson that Mr. James appropriates as authoritatively as blacksmiths, yard boys, and groundsmen dominated the sport of their masters. He sees no difference between their achievements and those of the Athenian athletes.

Portentous as this sounds, it is what Mr. James means by civilization. It is, for him, that sweetness of disposition and that clarity of intellect that Matthew Arnold defined as culture, and Mr. James's book dramatizes its ironies as accurately as Arnold or Henry Adams did, and does it not through contemplation but through action. He was a scorer at cricket matches in his younger days, and it is this job of numbering strokes, of adding up scores, that has given him a memory that can only be described as epical, not because the figures are there in the records, but because these figures that he describes are made to run and bowl and bat again. All the cricketing clichés apply: flanneled fools or flanneled warriors, they lope past, dive, are struck out for their folly, in his epic poem, the cricketer's *Iliad*.

"It's just a book about cricket, for God's sake." It isn't. It is a book about cricket for the gods' sake as well. It is a book about treachery, despair, and the fate of some of the best for being black, and still it is written without bitterness. Anger, yes, but no rancor. It is a noble book about poor, beautifully built, but socially desperate men (one of whom begged his captain to be allowed to play the game barefoot because shoes slowed down his delivery) who made this game the next thing to religion. Mr. James radiantly celebrates this blend of African prowess with Victorian codes. He sees how those Victorian ideals of gentlemanly conduct were ethics, even tribal ethics, regardless of race, and not a trap.

The empire that Mr. James, who was born in Trinidad in 1901, lived under, like Greece, had its slaves. He is one of their descendants. Like Rome, Britain sent out its governors, its consuls, its educators. But Mr. James was never blinded by the plaster casts and hypocritical marble copies of the Victorian ideal. He always had a hard mind, and this book does not try to make marble from ebony. It would be laughable if it were yet another paean of gratitude, a fake pastoral with classical echoes, but it would also be incredible, since Mr. James has been a Marxist (who has broken with Russia) and, in a politically active life, has been interned on Ellis Island, out of which degradation he wrote his *Mariners, Renegades and Castaways*; he has also been a pamphleteer, a pioneering West Indian novelist, and in "Black Jacobins" a historian of the Haitian revolution. All his life he has been known in the islands, by trade unionists as well as by writers, as a controversial humanist. But he loves cricket above everything else, not because it is a sport, but because he has found in it all the decencies required for a culture.

Then how can one be as passionate about the Russian Revolution as he is and still idealize a sport practiced by "gentlemen"? In his long life Mr. James has arrived, through this book, at a calm center. His calm is that of a meridian between two oceans, two cultures, even between radical and conservative politics, without mere neutrality. His calm is not neutrality. It has the passion of conviction, for decent conduct is the first and last thing required of men, as it is of states. He has arrived at that calm as quietly as a knight concludes a pilgrimage, and his quest has been that cup called The Ashes, that grail of Test Cricket for which teams from South Africa, New Zealand, Australia, Pakistan, India, and the West Indies have fought, so that one of their captains—many of them knighted later—could hold it up to the world.

It is Mr. James's belief that there is a difference between discipline and natural grace, between relentless practice and genius. But he cherishes obedience in the

Sophoclean sense, or even in the Roman way of not questioning the emperor's thumb of the umpire, if not of the empire. For him, obedience irradiates the most belligerent stroke-maker; he is appalled at the commercial anarchy of American sport. But things have changed. Cricket teams, through a certain entrepreneur, can now be bought or rented for high salaries, and black West Indian cricketers now play in South Africa. But it is the ideal that remains untarnished, not its vandals.

Mr. James's ancestors are African; why does he find mimesis in Periclean and not African sculpture when he describes the grace of his cricketers? Bodily movement is not a principle of African art, and the game is not played there on the scale of its other arenas. Proletarian in politics, patrician in taste, Mr. James should be a contradiction, but he was never a target for black radicals, rather one of its legislators, like Frantz Fanon, Léopold Sédar Senghor, Aimé Césaire, and Kwame Nkrumah. His history as a polemicist, his campaigns for African and West Indian nationalism have often caused him to be blacklisted, interned, and put under house arrest in his native Trinidad. And, in fact, if one thinks carefully again, *Beyond a Boundary* can be thought of as subversion; it undermines concepts that feel safe, it beats tradition by joining it, and its technique is not bitterness but joy.

Writers who worship a sport can sublimate their mediocrity into envy. Mr. James, who was a good bowler, has no envy. He sounds like a better bowler than Hemingway was a bullfighter or Mailer a boxer. He had real promise and was going to make cricketing his profession. He chortles with unaffected boasting about bowling out Learie Constantine, but what remains in this book is the shadow that stained the heroes of his boyhood with colonial prejudice—the darkening future when the "gentleman's game" is over, and his blacksmiths and roundsmen split from their teammates to go their own ways.

This sense of dusk in *Beyond a Boundary* provides it with history, gives it a tragic enchantment, since it is a chronicle of both the sport and the decline of an empire, from colonialism to independence, from the days when black and brown cricketers had different clubs to the days of the black captaincy of Frank Worrell. It is also a book, then, about twilight, about the turning of an epoch, and yet its tone is triumphal. Most of all, for a third of its length, it is like an excellent novel. Its characters are more than biographical asides. They have their own arc, no matter how minor their roles. Here is a "novella" in one paragraph that could have been written only by a mind confident of its width:

One year, Judith worked as usual from early morning in preparation for the day, doing everything that was needed. The friends came, the match was played and then all trooped in to eat, hungry, noisy and happy. Judith was serving when suddenly she sat down, saying, "I am not feeling so well." She leaned her head on the table. When they bent over to find out what was wrong she was dead. I would guess that she had been "not feeling well" for days, but she was not one to let that turn her aside from doing what she had to do.

Mr. James devoured Thackeray in his boyhood. He reread *Vanity Fair* so often that he would invite his school friends to open it at any page, and then he would give a précis of the contents of that page. In boyhood he came across this passage from a book on cricket and says, "I began to tingle":

Beldham was great in every hit, but his peculiar glory was the cut. Here he stood, with no man beside him, the laurel was all his own; it seemed like the cut of a racket. His wrist seemed to turn on springs of the finest steel.

This, understandably, might excite a boy wanting to be a great writer, but any boy today as keen on cricket as Mr. James was then would be already a writer if he appreciated this passage by Mr. James himself:

My grandfather went to church every Sunday morning at eleven o'clock wearing in the broiling sun a frock-coat, striped trousers and top-hat, with his walking stick in hand, surrounded by his family.

Fair enough, Victorian in metre, decorous in memory; then the right tingle comes: "The underwear of the women crackling with starch."

This is simply one stroke from a book whose light is as clear as a summer game's and which, as the highest tribute I can offer, every writer should read, because there, in one phrase, like the broken bottles on a moonlit wall in Chekhov, is the history of a colonial epoch: its rigours, its deprivations, and its pride.

(*1984*)

The Garden Path:
V. S. Naipaul

The summer jobs were done. The fallen aspens
about whose wide tangled spread of broken branches
grass and weeds had grown tall and dark,
a separate area of vegetation—
the fallen aspens were cut up with a chain-saw
and the cut-logs piled up in the back garden.

Press one foot on the soil of England and the phantoms spring. Poets, naturalists, novelists have harrowed and hallowed it for centuries with their furrowing pens as steadily as its yeomen once did with the plough. No other literature is so botanical as English, so seeded with delight and melancholy in the seasons, from "The Shepherd's Calendar" to Edward Thomas to those wistful prose poems that still appear on the editorial pages of English newspapers. Boundless as its empire became, England remained an island, a manageable garden to its poets, every one of whom is a pastoralist; and if now it has succumbed to the despair of Hamlet, "an unweeded garden that grows to seed / things rank and gross in nature" possessing it, or the malicious midden that is in Ted Hughes, still the provinciality of English poetry through Langland, Shake-

speare, Spenser, Milton, Marvell, Pope, Keats, Wordsworth, Hardy, the Georgians, Thomas, is its pride.

Culture and agriculture are synonyms over there. The
sense of England is not so much of setting out to see the
world as of turning one's back on it, of privacy, not adventure. The lines used as an epigraph above could have
been written by the phantom of Edward Thomas, or by
others: by Clare, Cobbett, Hardy, even a meticulous Georgian. They are from V. S. Naipaul's novel *The Enigma of
Arrival*, and they celebrate Wiltshire. They are his home-
coming, his devotions. But to those of us for whom his
direction has always been clear, this arrival is neither
enigmatic nor ironic but predictable. The final essay ex-
amination has been submitted, and the marks are in. Gentlemen, we now have among us another elegiac pastoralist,
an islander himself, the peer of Clare and Cobbett, not
only in style, but in spirit. And if the cost to that spirit
has meant virulent contempt towards the island of his origin, then rook, shaw, and hedgerow, tillage and tradition,
will soothe him, because although he may reject his own
soil, his own phantoms, the earth everywhere is forgiving,
even in Trinidad, and rejects no one.

When two long sections of Naipaul's book appeared
in *The New Yorker*, I cherished them as the tenderest writing Naipaul had ever done. Tempered and delicate, the
mood of these pieces had the subdued subtleties of the
weather their pliant sentences celebrated. They were pious
in their tribute, and close to glory, to that glory that in
Edward Thomas's poems brings us to tears in their natural
affections; and they had a bracing, springing rhythm, as
cool, as fresh, as pneumatic as moss underfoot. If there
was any enigma at all, it was that of astonishment, because
Naipaul was celebrating. There was no acidity in his pleasures, no ascetic tartness in this mellowing. Then the book
began to disfigure itself. The old distemper set in. The

elation and gratitude shrivelled and puckered and once again left the teeth on edge, the scour on the tongue.

The Enigma of Arrival calls itself a novel. But unless we are meant to take the novel to be the enigma of all autobiography—that everything recorded by the act of memory is inevitably a fiction, that in life there is no such thing as a hero because a hero presumes a plot—the book is negligible as a novel and crucial as autobiography. Or vice versa, if you like transparent puzzles. The chronology of events, the family names, the geography, all coincide with Naipaul's own; but as we read, mischievous uncertainty irritates us because of the suppression of those things that advance fiction: whether the narrator lived in total solitude in the Wiltshire countryside, and, if the narrator did, whether he avoided, for the sake of art, the temporary solaces of sex or marriage, whether he cooked for himself—because all this happens over years.

If the narrator's only companion was work, the hermitage is made admirable, but only in the way legends are—by a concentrated selfishness, by that self-canonization of the dedicated writer in a hostile world, the misunderstood, the displaced, the exiled, all of whom are becoming as corny as Dickensian orphans, because either every writer is an exile (not only this narrator-Naipaul) or no writer is. What keeps plot and excitement alive in *Robinson Crusoe* is not the myth of isolation but the challenge of endurance through ordinary objects, and through the vibrations of such objects the increase of loneliness, the growing scream inside the heart for companionship or, in another word, for love.

Here is where Naipaul's book sours, because the narrator is not interested in love. He falls neither in nor out of it, and this is a defeat he must accept if he is both narrator and Naipaul. The same lovers of gardens enslaved and finally ignored their empire once they had exhausted the soil that produced sugar for afternoon tea; and so, wondrously broad as the novel begins, it shallows into a fretful murmur, a melodious whine. Trinidad injured him. England saves him.

The book takes its title from a painting by de Chirico. A wharf. An empty city. A wanderer. A dangerous model already, and one that Naipaul has never used before: the art of someone else. More dangerous because surrealism, or metaphorical painting, is the imagination at its most second-rate. It is illustrated cliché: every arrival is a journey, etc. The surrealist tries to disturb us by upsetting formulas, then rigidifies his own. For time he gives us melting clocks, for phantasma, elephants on spiderish legs, hats floating without heads beneath them, infinite perspectives. The worst aspect of surrealism is that it requires so much labour to preserve the evanescent.

Naipaul does not go down that cul-de-sac; he is too much the rationalist, too deliberately commonsensical, too devoted to the parallel lines of history and reason to go after ambiguity, hallucination, and magic. But for the first time in his work we are thrilled by the temptation offered him, a temptation the narrator rejects, avoiding the seduction of writing a novel about that arrival in a hallucinatory port in the Roman Empire. Replace British for Roman, Naipaul for the traveller, the autobiography for the unwritten novel, and we have a neat trick, a prosaic irony. An aside, not a hymn. And this aside on the idea of history says simply that a man whose background was that of the degradation of indenture, of displacement, has used that background to master his craft, to move from servitude to certainty, and has found that certainty on the imperial soil of England.

The concept of English literature once belonged, naturally, to England. And, synonymously, to its power and its morality. It produced its books and exported them to the provinces. In those provinces the native writer absorbed the best of the language, but also the stuff that came with it, the power and the morals. It was this that magnetized Joseph Conrad, a provincial from the Third World of Poland under the peaks of the French, German, and British Empires. Naipaul has avoided this absorption with the suspicion of the servant. What is the cost to his Indianness of loving England (because that is what love of the English countryside means)? To whom does he owe any fealty? Ancestors? The surroundings that history placed them in, the cane fields of Trinidad, were contemptible, as they themselves would have to be, having lost both shame and pride. Therefore, the only dignity is to be neither master nor servant, to choose a nobler servitude: writing. The punishment for the choice is the astonishment of gratitude, to be grateful to the vegetation of an English shire. Not to India or the West Indies, but to the sweet itch of an old wound.

To detail the plot of this non-autobiography/non-novel would be to consider it by the very terms it avoids. If nothing happens in it, or rather, if what happens takes place across a fence, or on the far side of a field, that is in fact how life itself is: people betray each other as they do in this book, murder for jealousy, wither into old age, lose their jobs, while our own egocentricity absorbs other people's tragedies as interruptions or irritations. *The Enigma of Arrival* is mercilessly honest in its self-centredness, in its seasonal or eruptive sadnesses. It is as true as life, in the terrible sense that nothing really concerns us.

So what is observed by the narrator is oblique experience, seen and registered from the side of the eye, the parallel that is another's sorrow, until the end of the book, when the narrator's young sister dies and his grief blocks any sense of purpose. What is looked at—stream, hedge, deer—can be seen clearly, registered, and praised. But it can also be trusted to be itself, its variations not treacheries, its changes vitalizing. The early wonder of the book lies in the vigour of its stride, in its health. Year after healing year passes in the calendar that Naipaul calls his Book of Hours. His delight is treated with exactness, and the growth of pleasure draws the reader in without fancy. There isn't a better English around, and for me this is wonderful without bewilderment, since our finest writer of the English sentence, by praising the beauty of England, however threatened with industrial encroachment, preserves it from itself.

:

The best leaves of this book are touched by grace, and the wonder would have remained if the anonymity of the narrator had remained one with the landscape he cherishes. But the "I," the novelist in the autobiographer, moves from the present tense of lyric verse rhythms to the past tense of fiction, and the phantoms of the old Naipauline trauma—the genteel abhorrence of Negroes, the hatred of Trinidad, the idealization of History and Order—appear at the end of Naipaul's garden path. The self-assurance of the author's direction has to be fortified, dramatized, exaggerated, and so the author's lie begins. Here is Naipaul as an eighteen-year-old writer en route to England on his island scholarship. He is in New York, and this is how he remembers seeing the light:

Without the paper [a newspaper] I would not have known that the weather was unseasonable. But I did not need the paper to make me see the enchantment of the light. The light indoors in the hotel was like the light outdoors. The outdoor light was magical. I thought it was created by the tall buildings, which, with some shame, I stopped to look up at, to get their size. Light indoors flowed into light outdoors: the light here was one. In Trinidad, from seven or eight in the morning to five in the afternoon, the heat was great; to be out of doors was to be stung, to feel the heat and discomfort . . . The colors of the New York streets would have appeared to me, in Trinidad, as "dead" colors, the colors of dead things, dried grass, dead vegetation, earth, sand, a dead world—hardly colors at all.

To whom? Not to a painter. What happens in the summer in New York? Why is the sticky, insufferable humidity of any city summer preferable or more magical than the dry fierce heat of the Caribbean, which always has the startling benediction of breeze and shade? Why is this heat magical in Greece or in the desert, and just heat in Trinidad? We move easily from the climate to its people:

People had no news; they revealed themselves quickly. Their racial obsessions, which once could tug at my heart, made them simple people. Part of the fear of extinction which I had developed as a child had partly to do with this: the fear of being swallowed up or extinguished by the simplicity of one side or the other, my side or the side that wasn't mine.

It was odd: the place itself, the little island and its people, could no longer hold me. But the island—with the curiosity it had awakened in me for the larger world, the idea of civilization, and the idea of antiquity; and all the anxieties it had quickened in me—the island had given me the world as a writer.

Or, more honestly, "had given the world me as a writer." Nothing wrong with that. Despite his horror of being claimed, we West Indians are proud of Naipaul, and that is his enigmatic fate as well, that he should be so cherished by those he despises. But the estimate of his lonely journey towards becoming a writer is conservative. The statistics aren't fixed; they're ignored. His own island, a generation before, gave the world C.L.R. James (a Negro) and Samuel Selvon, and other islands offered the world George Lamming, Wilson Harris, Roger Mais, Jean Rhys, Edgar Mittelholzer, John Hearne, Shiva Naipaul, Jamaica Kincaid, scores of excellent short stories, the po-

ets Eric Roach, Cecil Herbert, George Campbell, Edward
Braithwaite, a few hundred calypsonians, Bob Marley,
Sparrow, Kitchener. But how weak Naipaul's struggle
would seem if it were communal; if his dedication was
seen to be shared; if what he felt in his youth was held to
be felt in common by thousands of young Asian, African,
Canadian, Australian writers from all the former provinces
of the empire: if more people knew *Beyond a Boundary*
and *The Black Jacobins* (by James), and *The Lonely Lon-
doners* and *Ways of Sunlight* (by Selvon), *In the Castle of
My Skin* (by Lamming), *The Palace of the Peacock* (by Wilson Harris), and so on. Naipaul moans about the fact that
in our youth the bookshelves of English literature were
lined with Penguins and Everymans, when in fact the islands had small but excellent libraries (since they could
only afford the classics). Still, he must perpetuate this
oblique deceit to appear as a marvel. For who would want
to attend a convention of Crusoes, a conference of hermits?

The myth of Naipaul as a phenomenon, as a singular,
contradictory genius who survived the cane fields and the
bush at great cost, has long been a farce. It is a myth he
chooses to encourage—though he alone knows why, since
the existence of other writers in no way diminishes his gift.
If he doesn't want to play, like the peevish sixth-grader
still contained in an almost great writer, he can go and
play by himself; but that is not going to stop the game.
Nobody draws more attention to himself than a conspicuous hermit; nobody is going to get more applause, more
solemn nods of respect. There is something alarmingly ve-
nal in all this dislocation and despair. Besides, it is not
true. There is, instead, another truth. It is Naipaul's prejudice.

Frankness doesn't absolve him of it. Of course prejudice comes from history, from the hoarded genealogy of
the tribe; yet if Naipaul's attitude towards Negroes, with

its nasty little sneers (injurer and injured can seek them out for themselves in this book), was turned on Jews, for example, how many people would praise him for his frankness? Who would have exalted that "honesty" for which he is praised as our only incorruptible writer from the Third World?

:

Victims are now as articulate as their oppressors, and this is not merely a matter of polemics. Prejudice taints the imaginations of Conrad, of Hemingway, of Greene, as much as it does the adventure novel; and it deserves to be judged with all the japes and apologies of gangs. Joyce, Shakespeare, Dante, for all their clear hatreds, are beyond this self-disfigurement. Naipaul's book, which began as a healing, is not an advance. *That* is its sadness, *that* is its disenchantment. There is the absence of all engima, for once again those abstract nouns History and Empire acquire a serenity equal to their alleged synonyms, Culture and Art. Over there in the lanes of England, these words survive and refresh.

If the world that Naipaul has left behind for others to care about has, for the descendants of slave and indentured worker, neither Art nor Culture, neither flower gardens nor venerable elms, it is because none of that was given to the slave or the indentured worker. To write about this lack as if it were the fault of the African and the Indian is not only to betray them but to lie. Naipaul is unfair. He is unjust. And he is unfair and unjust at an obscene cost, at the cost of those who do not have his eloquence, his style. Slavery and indenture were technological concepts, not aesthetic ones. They were part of the daily accountancy of a basically banal empire. But things have their price. The enigma or, more simply, the revenge, exacted by a belief in history is that the descendants of the enslaved will revere their servitude if it will lead them to those peaks of Art and Culture, to the heart of that empire, to its pastoral villas, manors, temples, and streets. This makes History and Empire worth all their suffering, if the suffering will produce Art. But the servant's present tense is not Naipaul's pluperfect. That tense has been refined, rewritten, judged, given an epic sweep, compressed into the precise yet still elegiac simplicity of this kind of epiphany:

I could see, in the documents of this later period, the lineaments of the world I had grown up in. Asian-Indian immigrants had come in the period of nineteenth-century torpor. As a schoolboy I had assumed that torpor to be a constant, something connected with the geographical location of the island, the climate, the quality of the light. It had never occurred to me that the drabness I knew had been man-made, that it had causes, that there had been other visions, and indeed other landscapes there.

What is this but style without truth? What sort of torpor? And for a hundred years? One had imagined that the nineteenth century was a bit more energetic—if not in industry, at least in art. And how much torpor were slave and indentured worker allowed? Yet in the pluperfect tense of the twentieth century, the descendant of the indentured can elegize the torpor of the nineteenth. Naipaul is talking about the torpor of the intellect, not about anything as ordinary as work.

One sighs and proceeds to:

This empire explained my birth in the New World, the language I used, the vocation and ambition I had; this empire in the end explained my presence there in the valley, in the cottage, in the grounds of the manor.

This is modest enough to be messianic. But the empire also explained the birth of hundreds of thousands of immigrants, of the language they use, of their vocations and their ambitions, of their presence in valley and cottage on a manor ground, in Brixton and elsewhere.

    :

Naipaul tires of racism in Trinidad and returns home to Britain. Not to the Britain of Paki-bashing, or of the race riots of Brixton, but to the comforts of its countryside. This may strike the average mind as the equivalent of a Soviet dissident going home to Gorky, of a thirties Jew finding rest in Berlin, of a Bantu celebrating the delights of Johannesburg. Perhaps the Pakis and the black Brits brought hatred on themselves, as so many Third World countries in Naipaul's travel books have brought about their own psychic collapse by attempting to compete with their former empires. The horror in these books, from *The Middle Passage* through *Eva Perón and the Killings in Trinidad* to *Finding the Center*, is the horror encountered in bush frontiers, in the pseudo-cities of Latin America, India, and the Middle East, but never in the central horrors of our century: the concentration camps, the forced-labour camps of Soviet Russia, their scale so much larger than many Caribbean islands, those archipelagoes of calculated, refined social science.

There is the real enigma: that the provincial, the colonial, can never civilize himself beyond his province, no matter how deeply he immures himself in the woods of a villa outside Rome or in the leafy lanes of Edwardian England. And that is not pathetic; it is glorious. It is the other thing that is the final mimicry: to achieve absorption into what is envied not because that absorption is the dissolution of individuality, the sort of blessed anonymity that Hinduism teaches, but because it is only the vain mutter of "I have survived."

As beautiful as the prose becomes in the first chapters of this novel, it is scarred by scrofula, by passages from which one would like to avert one's eye; and these reveal, remorselessly, Naipaul's repulsion towards Negroes. It is a physical and historical abhorrence that, like every prejudice, disfigures the observer, not his object. To cite examples would reduce the critic to the role of defender or of supplicant, would expose him to more of Naipaul's scorn. That self-disfiguring sneer that is praised for its probity is only that: a wrinkling of the nostrils, a bemused crinkling of the eyes at the antics of mimicking primates, at their hair, at their voices, at their hands extended in the presumption of intimacy.

In the twentieth century, the languages of all the tribes can sound like a Babel, and that sound can terrify the secondary genius. Therefore, that genius hoards itself and its tribal language, convincing itself that amid the echolalia of screaming victims and confessional apologists it must immure itself in the sacred, priestly dedication of being "a writer," but cautiously keeping both callings distinct: writer and priest. Thus the writer becomes his own confessor. He blesses or curses or absolves himself by the rites of his writing, preserving his secularity, his public, his profitable mask.

Shantih to his pen, though, and a benediction on the peace that has come to him after the exhaustions of a world whose features he has still described more honestly than most. In a small hillside hotel whose back verandah looks out on a serenity of pasture, saddle ridge, grazing cattle, and a view of the Caribbean between its bushy hills, I found an appropriate blessing under the photograph of a sadhu in an old *National Geographic*: "Renouncing possessions, sadhus are life-long pilgrims. For such a holy man, said the god Indra, patron of travelers: 'All his sins are destroyed by his fatigues in wandering.'" That is how I prefer to end—to cherish the narrator of *The Enigma of Arrival*, not as an enigmatic English squire who has finally arrived, but as the sadhu that he might have become. Peace to the traveller, and calm to the mind growing nearer to that radiance, to the vision that sees all earth as sacred, including his birthplace, and all people as valuable, including Trinidadians.

(1987)

Magic Industry:
Joseph Brodsky

I

"August," a Russian émigré poet explained to me, "is a man in Russian language," "so when you say in your poem 'The housemaid, August' . . ." He groaned. In Russian, the months have gender. Nouns have masculine or feminine endings, but unless they are personified, the months are simply nouns. Of course, in the pastoral tradition there were traditional personifications for the months. May was feminine, a white girl in a white dress in a meadow of white flowers; June vibrated with the furled thunder of the rose, with the opening hearts of its lovers; December was a hoary, icicle-bearded ancient. But these personifications were a calendar's images, and not grammar. If August, in Russian, was a man, what was he to this exiled poet? A wheat-haired worker with a pitchfork on a revolutionary poster?

I had seen August as a housemaid-cook, her ebony head in a white kerchief as she whipped sheets from a clothesline in a house near the sea, the way that storms, in the hurricane month, whip sails from the Caribbean horizon. In the rasp of the month's sound there was the rustle of dry grass as well as the gusting of laundry and the sibilance of surf, but if the English word were to shift its shadow to the Russian landscape, to its imagined summer, I could personify it as either man or woman. August, the man, could have been one of those bored, idle intellectuals in Chekhov's plays, with a voice as lulling and finally as soporific as its leaves, but August was also Nina in *The Seagull*, a girl like a cabbage-white butterfly attaching herself to Trigorin's elbow, by a stunned lake. It was impossible for me to understand Mikhail's anguish or exasperation over the name of a month, but it is one of the desolations that accompany translation.

   :

Joseph Brodsky's volume *To Urania* protracts this challenge line by line, phrase by phrase, syllable by syllable. Of course every conscientious translator endures this challenge, but one feels that Brodsky wishes the book to be read as English verse, not as translated Russian. This has its difficulties, its knots, but one is grateful that the knots are there, that the rough nap of the lines is not smoothed over by the flirtation of an even English diction, that kind of fatal levelling that has so often made his compatriots, Pasternak and Tsvetayeva, and even as tough a poet as Mandelstam, acquire in translation the sheen and gloss of greeting cards. The kind of translation that turns Doctor Zhivago into Omar Sharif.

> *The month of stalled pendulums. Only a fly in August*
> *in a dry carafe's throat is droning its busy hymn.*

This is from Brodsky's "Roman Elegies II," in his own translation.* The fly, of course, is not "in" August, but August itself. The insect personifies the month, but it does so without gender. In English the sound is androgynous,

---

* *Unless otherwise indicated, all translations are by Brodsky.*

the sex of the housefly, unlike that of the housemaid, is not identified or important. What the translator is after is the simultaneity of assonances that breed from the rasp and hiss of the English noun. The somnolence that is underlined by the insect's industry, the buzz contained in the sounds "busy" and "its," the distorted echo of "hymn" from "pendulums," the effort required from the very beginning of the line to extend "the" into "month," all of which, magisterially, and in an adopted language, establish torpor. Even the throat of the carafe contains a dusty echo, that of the dry throat of the reader within which the sound of the insect's buzz is stirring. And now one wonders if the original Russian is as rich in its consonantal sibilance as Brodsky's English, and not the other way around.

This is not only admirable but astonishing.

:

For a poet to translate himself involves not only a change of language but what translation literally means, a crossing to another place, an accommodation of temperament, a shadowing of sensibility as the original poem pauses at the frontier where every proffered credential must be carefully, even cruelly, examined, and not by a friendly or inimical authority, but by the author himself. This is an ordinary experience, if one thinks of the original verse as being merely an equivalent rendered by interlinears, then heightened, touched up, like a fake passport photo. What is extraordinary, in fact phenomenal in its effort, is the determination to render, almost to deliver, the poem from its original language into the poetry of the new country. To give the one work, simultaneously, two mother tongues.

The prodigious labour involved in this collection of Brodsky's would be impressive enough, since Brodsky is a complex and demanding poet, if these poems were merely responsibly, even beautifully, translated, but they are not so much translated as re-created, by Brodsky himself, an achievement that makes him an even greater poet than we shruggingly acknowledge him to be. A great modern Russian poet, an heir of Mandelstam, is plenty for one man to be in his lifetime, but to have re-created from the original Russian a poem as spacious, as botanically precise, as delightful in it rhymes as his "Eclogue V: Summer," and then to think of Edmund Spenser's ghost rustling behind its pages, to recall Keats and Clare in their own language, is more than a technical feat of adaptation. There is, for one reader, no yearning for the original Russian, no sense of vacancy, of something lost or not rendered. It is the industry of magic.

IV

Summer twilight's fluttering window laces!
Cold cellars packed with milk jugs and lettuce,
a Stalin or a Khrushchev on the latest
news, jammed by cicadas' incessant rattle:
homemade bilberry jelly jars bat the rafters;
lime socks round apple orchards' ankles

look the whiter the darker it gets, like joggers
running beyond what the distance offers;
and farther still loom the real ogres
of full-size elms in the evening's bluing.

—*"Eclogue V: Summer" (translated by George L. Kline and the poet)*

What is even more admirable is Brodsky's determination to continue, to hallow by his reverence, the history of his craft, its sacred, tested shapes in various languages, through Virgil as well as Spenser, in ode as well as eclogue, and also in the solid, elaborate architecture of his stanzas. George L. Kline is the co-translator of "Eclogue V: Summer," but anyone who has worked with Brodsky translating Brodsky knows that what the original goes through is a chaos of transformation. So the labour proceeds in three stages, with which the fellow translator must keep pace: the first is the interlinear translation, the second a transformation, and the third, with luck and with Brodsky's tireless discipline, transfiguration.

:

How is the genius of another language induced? It is induced through admiration, by that benign envy which all poets have for the great poets of a different language, and this admiration may be perpetuated through memory, through recitation, through translation, and by having models which it can use for its own development in both tongues. Brodsky is a poet in exile, not a novelist or scientist. He, like Pasternak, translated several modern American and English poets, as well as John Donne, and yet when he chooses to write a poem in English like his elegy for Robert Lowell, there is nothing that one could point to as being derivative of or indebted to other writers, including Auden.

> *In the autumnal blue*
> *of your church-hooded New*
> *England, the porcupine*
> *sharpens its golden needles*
> *against Bostonian bricks*
> *to a point of needless*
> *blinding shine.*

Whenever Brodsky sounds like Auden it is not in imitation but in homage, and the homage is openly confessed. What his English writing does, rather, is to pay its tribute to a language which he loves as much as his own Russian, and it is the love of that language which has expanded his spiritual biography, not with the hesitancy of an émigré, but with a startling exuberance. This is the happiness which he has earned from exile.

Mandelstam, Pasternak, Tsvetayeva, Akhmatova, Mayakovsky, whatever Russia has done to them, remain in Russia, in the language of their native land. Brodsky's case is different. The body language of a dancer does not need translation, nor do the formulas of a scientist; the power of a novel is comprehended through plot and character, but the grafting of the poetic instinct onto a politically disembodied, disenfranchised trunk, of a mind with no luggage but memory, requires an energy which must first astonish itself.

Grammar is a form of history, and Brodsky the self-translator knows that. Because he is a poet, not a novelist, he is not concerned with the action in a sentence, the history that is released by grammar, but with what action grows from the approaching syllable, regardless of the gender of a Russian month, or moth. If some critic of Brodsky's work says "This isn't English," the critic is right in the wrong way. He is right in the historical, the grammatical sense, by which I do not mean grammatical errors but a given grammatical tone. This is not "plain American, which dogs and cats can read," the barbarous, chauvinistic boast of the poet as mass thinker, as monosyllabic despot; but the same critic, in earlier epochs, might have said the same thing about Donne, Milton, Browning, Hopkins.

There is a sound to Brodsky's English that is peculiarly his, and this sound is often one of difficulty. I should have written "the most honest kind of difficulty," because there are varieties of honesty in poets, variations that can become, as Auden ravaged his own style to excise them, lies.

:

The other easy dismissal is to call difficulty "metaphysical," as well as, of course, to ascribe obscurity to a fault of translation. But Donne is a poet who also translates himself, who shows us, as he lays siege to meaning, the progress of that siege. Brodsky does the same:

Thus, prey to speeds
of light, heat, cold, or darkness,
a sphere in space without markers
spins and spins.

—*"Seven Strophes" (translated by Paul Graves)*

or:

Petulant is the soul begging mercy from
an invisible or dilated frame.
Still, if it comes to the point where the blue acrylic
dappled with cirrus suggests the Lord,
say, "Give me strength to sustain the hurt,"
and learn it by heart like a decent lyric.

—*"Sextet"*

I I

Brodsky's models, Ovid, the Virgil of the *Georgics*, Pro-
pertius, even Pindar in his large ode "Lithuanian Nocturne," are defiantly archaic; a modern poet might argue
that they are even presumptuously, perversely, so. In an
age which, still nauseous from the backwash of modern-
ism, from the upheavals of Pound, Eliot, and Williams,
confuses the classic with the antique, which juxtaposes
the normal or abnormal life next to an ideal but inert past,
Brodsky resists the elegiac seductions of ruins. Instead, he
coarsens their atmosphere with the belligerence of a bar-
barian from the steppes or forests or wooden towns of an
earlier Russia. He chews and swallows the past audibly.
He compares his ruined teeth to the Parthenon; his statues are stripped of their fig leaves, they have crotches; but
of course this vulgarity is an act. Better this, though, than
wishing the past would go away, or that, as Eliot and

Pound in their Byronic romanticism did, it could come back. Brodsky's thrushes sing in the "hairdo" of a cypress. Besides, his landscape is not a row of broken columns against a blue sea; it is not a tribal, ancestral desert. It is the width of rural Russia in the dusk.

Every poet has a particular twilight in his soul, and for Brodsky it is not a wine-darkening sea, over which he grieves for the setting sun of a classical empire, but for that moment from which elegies are sprung by the tuning fork of sky and horizon; what one hears in his pages is the rough sound of a coniferous forest as the pennons of its triangular trees become silhouettes and enter night.

> *Evening in the Empire,*
> *in a destitute province. A conifer force*
> *wades the Neman and, bristling with darkening lances,*
> *takes old three-storied Kaunas . . .*

> —*"Lithuanian Nocturne"*

Or the landscape may whiten in obliterating snow, as the thick forest greys from its thicket of Cyrillics into the whiteness of the page itself, in which the voice of the poet hoarsens to a whisper.

> *That's the birth of an eclogue. Instead of the shepherd's*
> *   signal,*
> *a lamp's flaring up. Cyrillic, while running witless*
> *on the pad as though to escape the captor,*
> *knows more of the future than the famous sibyl:*
> *of how to darken against the whiteness,*
> *as long as the whiteness lasts. And after.*

> —*"Eclogue IV: Winter"*

:

Democracies are tyrannical about their art. The safest art ensures the perpetuity of the republic, the surveillance of, or the rewarding of, high mediocrity, and for Brodsky, who has written under two self-idealizing democracies, America and Soviet Russia, the role of the émigré can only continue to darken, not simply because he glorifies neither, but because he seems to be inhabiting his own country, muttering a complicated monologue which does not simplify its references, and whose spirit seems not to lament but to cherish disinheritance. His wanderings have neither a Holy nor an Agnostic Land, in other words, an Ego. He would be a lesser poet if he capitalized on his biography— a Russian Jew, an American Russian, a classical modernist—and that ego, openly, infuriatingly does not do the easy thing of saying *"Non serviam,"* because *"Non serviam"* is the ego's melodrama. Instead, it rejects anger, it does not flatter the torturer or the system with blame, nor has it rushed into the lowered arms of the Statue of Liberty because it may be afraid of being burnt by her torch. And a final irony is that Brodsky's ego is anonymous: this is what makes it classical. Not nobly so, because the voice whines and bitches, defines its owner often as a balding grumbler, an irascible guest.

> *These days evening sun still blinds the tenements' domino.*
> *But those who have loved me more than themselves are no*
> *longer alive. The bloodhounds, having lost their quarry,*
> *with vengeance devour the leftovers—herein their very*
>
> *strong resemblance to memory, to the fate of all things. The*
> * sun*
> *sets. Faraway voices, exclamations like "Scum!*
> *Leave me alone!"—in a foreign tongue, but it stands to rea-*
> * son.*
> *And the world's best lagoon with its golden pigeon*

coop gleams sharply enough to make the pupil run.
At the point where one can't be loved any longer, one,
resentful of swimming against the current and too perceptive
of its strength, hides himself in perspective.

—*"In Italy"*

:

Something of a sour Byron, smart enough to predict the
tricks of bureaucratic power, wanders through the cities
of *To Urania*. The impression, for a while, is reinforced by
the metre, the long lines with feminine endings and with
an echo of the triple rhymes of their original Russian,
which do not have the narrative rush of *Don Juan* but are
more relaxed, like the Clough of "Amours de Voyage." Yet
the whiff of sourness fades. There is no wine on the
breath, no sense of getting drunk on the deliverance of
exile. The translated Russian risks, in its usually hexametrical rhyming design, a metre which English associates
with the comic, the parodic, or the ironic. There is no
modern English or American poet who will take such
risks—being utterly serious with feminine endings, of attempting to reach the sublime and noble without the
pseudo-humility of the dying fall, the retractable conceit.
Double rhymes and long lines threaten contemporary poets in English with the bespectacled shade of Ogden Nash,
not to mention the garrulous precision of Byron. Wit has
therefore gone the way of rhyme. Metaphysical wit, as per
Eliot's essay on Donne, is something every modern poet
has attempted, but in most of this verse there is no history of poetry, no sense of epigrammatic parenthesis; in
fact, the parenthesis becomes the subject of the modern
poem.

Most contemporary verse is a poetry of asides, most
modern poems could be in parentheses. The intellectual
vigour of Brodsky's poetry is too alarming even for his

144 / Derek Walcott

poet-readers, because it contains the history of the craft, because it openly reveres its inheritance, but—and here comes the payoff—this wit is founded on what poets used to advance the craft by—intelligence, argument, an awareness of contemporary science, and not so much a sense of the past as a certainty that the past is always parsed in the present tense. This is why he has made himself such an ample poet; one feels that he has written these many poems, most of them very long, because they serve as a bulwark, a fortress against the modern. Such an intelligence needs bulk as much as it needs particulars. It is a system of accumulating asides, of progressive observations, and not only through metaphor but through the consequences of metaphor, the contradiction which metaphor can create. It can never be beautiful in the expected sense, in the same way that Donne's poems can be ugly.

This is the murderous example that Brodsky has set for the vocation. He shows us what casual, and therefore vain, intellects we are. He returns discipline to what it should be, creative agony. And he would have done this without the props of autobiography, without the international drama of his banishment.

:

The drama of exile passes: it has been, for Brodsky, exploitative on either side, the country that banishes and the country that takes the banished in. The drama passes, and there is the pain, not the theatricality of it. Parents die, grief shatters, the tyrant is faceless, the new evil is the clerk who passes on the request to another clerk—no guilt, facelessness, the zeros of faces that contain no personal responsibility or original sin. What country is left them? The mother tongue. The mother landscape, seen beyond tears as simply herself in the very way in which the exile, rising, eating, writing, reflects her.

The thought of you is receding like a chambermaid given
   notice.
No! like a railway platform, with block-lettered DVINSK
   or TATRAS.
But odd faces loom in, shivering and enormous,
also terrains, only yesterday entered into the atlas,
thus filling up the vacuum. None of us was well suited
for the status of statues. Probably our blood vessels
lacked in hardening lime. "Our family," you'd have put it,
"gave the world no generals, or—count our blessings—
great philosophers." Just as well, though: the Neva's surface
can't afford yet another reflection, brimming with
   "mediogres."
What can remain of a mother with all her saucepans
in the perspective daily extended by her son's progress?

—*"In Memoriam"*

And the agony sharpens when one knows that the mother
is both the poet's natural mother and his native Russia.
The son's progress is also Russia's.

   :

In "Lithuanian Nocturne" Brodsky writes to another exile.
He claims the Russian earth as a dimension beyond re-
gimes, beyond the sorrow he shares with his exile friend
Thomas Venclova.

XI

There are places in which
things don't change. These are a substitute
for one's memory. These are the acid
triumphs of fixative. There each mile
puts striped bars into focus . . .

A silent, open-mouthed evening sky breathes over the fur-
rows of the stanza.

V

Evening in the Empire,
in a destitute province. A conifer force
wades the Neman and, bristling with darkening lances,
takes old three-storied Kaunas; a blush of remorse
sweeps the stucco as darkness advances,
and the cobblestones glisten like bream in a net.

The poem advances darkly, muttering like a river, and it concludes without a seraphic burst of cornets from the clouds, without the pantheistic sentimentality into which it could have declined by its tone; ascending, instead, it has the steady drone of truth, which tempts the hearer to learn it by heart.

XXI

In the sky
far above the Lithuanian hills
something sounding like a prayer
for the whole of mankind, droning cheerlessly, drifts
toward Kurshskaya Point. This is St. Casimir's
and St. Nicholas's mumbling in their unattainable lair
where, minding the passage of darkness, they sift
hours. Muse! from the heights where you
dwell, beyond any creed's stratosphere, from your rarefied ether,
look, I pray you, together
with those two,
after these pacified sunken plains' sullen bard.
Do not let handmade darkness envelop his rafter.
Post your sentinels in his back yard.
Look, Urania, after
both his home and his heart.

The first poem in *To Urania*, "May 24, 1980," has gone out of the range of such fury as it might arouse from the center of the empire. The nomadic Jew is out there alone on his desert, and what infuriates both the professional Jew and the professional Jew-baiter is that the expelled should enjoy the desert. "May 24, 1980" is a birthday poem. It is a jeremiad with jokes. The exile recoils from the collective moan of the race.

> *I have braved, for want of wild beasts, steel cages,*
> *carved my term and nickname on bunks and rafters,*
> *lived by the sea, flashed aces in an oasis,*
> *dined with the-devil-knows-whom, in tails, on truffles.*
> *From the height of a glacier I beheld half a world, the earthly*
> *width. Twice have drowned, thrice let knives rake my nitty-*
> *gritty.*
> *Quit the country that bore and nursed me.*
> *Those who forgot me would make a city,*
> *I have waded the steppes that saw yelling Huns in saddles,*
> *worn the clothes nowadays back in fashion in every quarter,*
> *planted rye, tarred the roofs of pigsties and stables,*
> *guzzled everything save dry water.*

"Those who forgot me would make a city." Leaving Russia with a bottle of vodka and no visible future, and watching from the plane as, in a phrase from an earlier poem, "cities went dark as caviar," the poem ends with the exile retching, of having "brown clay . . . crammed down my larynx." Irreverence such as this is an irritation to any state or race.

Brodsky would have been banished from Augustan Rome, not merely from Soviet Russia, and one feels that, in his heart, he now prefers exile. The farthest exile is death.

:

Brodsky's poems are seamed with a sense of mortality. Time frays the flesh, unstitches veins, but no soul steps out of the body's crumpled, abandoned garment, trembling with lightness and transparency like a butterfly. Unlike his mentor Donne, he remains in the one dimension that he knows, however much he may be baffled by it, that of experience, of a futureless present tense, one without resurrection, without prophesy. Sonnet and sennet trumpet belief, from the overtures of Donne's opening lines, like a passage past a magnificent tapestry:

Since I am comming to that Holy roome,
. . .
Death be not proud, though some have called thee
Mighty and dreadfull . . .

At the round earths imagin'd corners, blow
Your trumpets, Angells . . .

Centuries later the rational dialectic of our modern empires, those of the West and the Eastern one, has made such faith merely literature, made poetry as archaic as tapestries, magnificent but not the truth. But neither poetry nor the Past is a decoration hung on a wall, not only in Brodsky's view, but in his body. Illness overshadows his page, and yet the verse shows no panic. In fact, the solid architecture of his stanzaic designs, the intricate triple rhymes, are solid, concrete, without a single heart flutter of doubt about their vocation.

Yet, without longing, these poems also contain angels, seraphs, not with the idealization of Rilke's beings, but as factual presences, as skaters in white battle uniforms, as rustles behind draperies, or as just statues. Brodsky's mind enters the statues without any prayer to transfigure them. Seraphs and kettles become commonplace in the house of the mind, and in the weather outside,

As though the mercury's under its tongue, it won't
talk. As though with the mercury in its sphincter,
immobile, by a leaf-coated pond
a statue stands white like a blight of winter.

After such snow, there is nothing indeed: the ins
and outs of centuries, pestered heather.
That's what coming full circle means—
when your countenance starts to resemble weather,
when Pygmalion's vanished. And you are free
to cloud your folds, to bare the navel.
Future at last! That is, bleached debris
of a glacier amid the five-lettered "never."
Hence the routine of a goddess, née
alabaster, that lets roving pupils gorge on
the heart of the color and temperature of the knee.
That's what it looks like inside a virgin.

—*"Galatea Encore" (written in English)*

A butterfly alights on the cannon of a tank and its trembling vanes may seem more fragile, but only in one proportion, because butterflies can survive rainstorms by their
pliancy of adaptation, by the surrender of their nature to
natural force, whereas tanks can be mired in their own
weight. This is the strength of modern Russian poetry, that
its poets have the contradiction of butterflies alighting on
cannons, that their fragility, confronting the armament of
the Soviet machine, is not elusive or fanciful but the natural utterance of its immense meadows, its serrated forests. A butterfly on barbed wire is Mandelstam's poetry,
Akhmatova's is one that flutters at the base of the prison
wall where she visits her son; one can add even the closed
wings of Tsvetayeva, who hanged herself, and by that miserable act released her soul. Through them Russia remains
provincial, and provinciality is the natural truth of every
poetry.

There they are, blueberry-laden forests,
rivers where the folk with bare hands catch sturgeon
or the towns in whose soggy phone books

you are starring no longer; farther eastward surge on
brown mountain ranges; wild mares carousing
in tall sedge; the cheekbones get yellower
as they turn numerous. And still farther east, steam
    dreadnoughts or cruisers,
and the expanse grows blue like lace underwear.

—"To Urania"

The warships are like tanks whose tracks are their wake, and a distant, incurious heartland, its wheeling horses and blueberry bushes, ignore them. Russia is too wide to accommodate the limits of any regime, and butterflies, anyway, are closer to the earth.

Touch me—and you'll touch dry burdock stems,
the dampness intrinsic to evenings in late Marchember,
the stone quarry of cities, the width of steppes,
those who are not alive but whom I remember.

—"Afterword" (translated by Jamey Gambrell and the poet)

This is the butterfly that alights on the tank turret in Afghanistan, but that is also borne along by the tank which is the weight, the slough, the steady heave and lumbering movement in Brodsky's hugely designed poems. The wide tracks laid behind their passage are not smooth. Their weight sometimes stalls, groans, grinding gears, pushing through brambles of semicolons. We heave, rest, and push with the lines, but they always emerge clear. They have chosen their difficult terrain.

:

It is this weight, width, determinedness of direction that poets in various languages admire in Brodsky, an example on a heroic scale, his self-conscription, his daily soldiering with no army behind him except the phantoms of the race's greatest poets, from any epoch which calls out to him. His country cannot abandon him any more than Augustan poetry could exile Ovid. He has his unchangeable Russia, and it is from her, from the tenderness of her children, Tsvetayeva, Akhmatova, the emaciation of Mandelstam, that his lyrics touch us with their strength, their fragility and comradeship.

> One more Christmas ends
> soaking stripes and stars.
> All my Polish friends
> are behind steel bars,
> locked like zeroes in
> some graph sheet of wrath:
> as a discipline
> slavery beats math.
>
>   . . .
>
> Deeper than the depth
> of your thoughts or mine
> is the sleep of death
> in the Vujek mine;
> higher than your rent
> is that hand whose craft
> keeps the others bent—
> as though photographed.
>
> Powerless is speech.
> Still, it bests a tear
> in attempts to reach,
> crossing the frontier,
> for the heavy hearts
> of my Polish friends.
> One more trial starts.
> One more Christmas ends.

—"A Martial Law Carol" (written in English)

Not all the poems in *To Urania* have been translated by Brodsky. Because he is such a demanding and expansive poet, we are grateful for the considerable labour, and in many cases the loving precision and anonymity of Harry Thomas's "Gorbunov and Gorchakov," a forty-page poem rerendered in stanzaic rhyme, as well as for the work of Jamey Gambrell, Jane Ann Miller, George L. Kline, Alan Myers, and Peter France. His translators have blended into the temperament of the volume without adding idiosyncrasies of their own, and the fact that *To Urania* has such a unified hum testifies to their transparency. Granted that there is no poem here with that miracle of adaptation which Richard Wilbur achieved with "Six Years Later" in Brodsky's preceding volume, *A Part of Speech*, yet that collection had the not necessarily desirable variety of an anthology of Brodsky seen through the eyes of contemporary American poets. *To Urania* is more of a whole, and it is this that enriches not only its native literature but that of the country in which a demonstrably great poet, an almost sublime intelligence, moves us and moves among us in the guise of another citizen.

(*1988*)

The Master of the Ordinary: Philip Larkin

I

The average face, the average voice, the average life—that is, the life most of us lead, apart from film stars and dictators—had never been defined so precisely in English poetry until Philip Larkin. He invented a muse: her name was Mediocrity. She was the muse of the diurnal, of habit, of repetition. She lived in life itself, not as a figure beyond it, a phantom of yearning, but as the plain, transparent companion of a confirmed benedict.

"Benedict" seems better than "bachelor" when we think of Larkin because of the word's monkish associations, suggesting his medieval patience in waiting for the right phrase to come, as well as what seemed to his readers to be a willful self-immolation as a librarian in Hull—since nothing sounds more ordinary, more mediocre than that. Increasingly silent as his last years passed, he seemed pleased to encourage this image of himself—Larkin the librarian, a bookworm smothering itself in a silken silence. Obviously, if Hull was all there was to life, if work was a cold toad that squatted on his heart, and if excitement and enthusiasm were dismissed as suspicious spasms, we were not to expect anything more radiant than this poem, as brief and frighteningly funny in its Keystone Kop ending as its topic:

> *What are days for?*
> *Days are where we live.*
> *They come, they wake us*
> *Time and time over.*
> *They are to be happy in . . .*

"They are to be happy in." God as a nanny, God as a schoolmaster, a parson, a constable:

> *Where can we live but days?*
>
> *Ah, solving that question*
> *Brings the priest and the doctor*
> *In their long coats*
> *Running over the fields.*
>
> —"Days"

And this:

> *For nations vague as weed,*
> *For nomads among stones,*
> *Small-statured cross-faced tribes*
> *And cobble-close families*
> *In mill-towns on dark mornings*
> *Life is slow dying.*
>
> —"Nothing to Be Said"
>
> *Life is first boredom, then fear.*
> *Whether or not we use it, it goes,*

And leaves what something hidden from us chose,
And age, and then the only end of age.

—*"Dockery and Son"*

A shudder and a nod from the reader. Is this catharsis? Spiritual redemption? You mean that's it?

　　:

If so, then what is it in Larkin that has made his collected poems a bestseller in Great Britain? Thirty-five thousand copies two months after publication last autumn. As the shade of a popular hermit, Larkin might say, bemused by the irony that nothing sells writing better than the writer's death, that there is a small fortune to be made in conspicuous isolation, that books may be "a load of crap," but they keep being read, borrowed, stolen, indexed, and bought. The fate he seemed to prefer, that of being remaindered and neglected because for him there was "nothing to be said," has been resoundingly contradicted by the size of his following, which numerically must be the equivalent of an audience at a rock concert. Even *The Whitsun Weddings* and the last short book, *High Windows*, had a large audience.

But has that fate been contradicted or confirmed? If his large readership consists mostly of average persons leading average lives, this is not because Larkin pitched his tone to accommodate them, the way that other popular poets, like Kipling, Frost, Betjeman, or Stevie Smith, did. His life, on the surface, was not exemplary. There was nothing to be envied in it. Partly it is patriotism that makes Larkin popular. Not a jingoistic bitterness lamenting the loss of England's power, not even his mockery of that power, but something gentle and piercingly sweet that tells the sad truths of ordinariness, as the poems of one of his models, Edward Thomas, do. An unread predecessor often opens the way to popularity for this apprentice. So Larkin's popularity is not only his but owes much to Thomas. This is Thomas's "Aspens":

> All day and night, save winter, every weather,
> Above the inn, the smithy, and the shop,
> The aspens at the cross-roads talk together
> Of rain, until their last leaves fall from the top.

And here is early Larkin:

> On shallow slates the pigeons shift together,
> Backing against a thin rain from the west
> Blown across each sunk head and settled feather,
> Huddling round the warm stack suits them best.

—"Pigeons"

There is in Larkin, in poems like "The Whitsun Weddings," a Georgian decency that is aware of England's smallness, and keeps the poem no wider than the rail lines of the metre in his many poems of departure. But departure for what? Never abroad, always England, an England that is quietly loved, just as it is in Thomas, and in a way beyond the architectural nostalgia of Betjeman:

> Coming up England by a different line
> For once, early in the cold new year,
> We stopped, and, watching men with number-plates
> Sprint down the platform to familiar gates,
> "Why, Coventry!" I exclaimed. "I was born here."
>
> I leant far out, and squinnied for a sign
> That this was still the town that had been "mine"

So long, but found I wasn't even clear
Which side was which. From where those cycle-crates
Were standing, had we annually departed . . .

—"I Remember, I Remember"

This empty street, this sky to blandness scoured,
This air, a little indistinct with autumn
Like a reflection, constitute the present—
A time traditionally soured,
A time unrecommended by event.

—"Triple Time"

Or, without abashment, the hymnal metre of:

And that will be England gone,
The shadows, the meadows, the lanes,
The guildhalls, the carved choirs.
There'll be books; it will linger on
In galleries; but all that remains
For us will be concrete and tyres.

—"Going, Going"

Larkin is like a retractable Kipling, whose empire is reduced to the diurnal familiarity of "canals with floatings of industrial froth," of

The large cool store selling cheap clothes
Set out in simple sizes plainly
(Knitwear, Summer Casuals, Hose,
In browns and greys, maroon and navy) . . .

—"The Large Cool Store"

And:

> . . .
>
> *a harsh-named halt, that shields*
> *Workmen at dawn; swerving to solitude*
> *Of skies and scarecrows, haystacks, hares and pheasants,*
> *And the widening river's slow presence,*
> *The piled gold clouds, the shining gull-marked mud . . .*

—*"Here"*

I have no idea how many times I have read the poems in *The Whitsun Weddings, High Windows*, and, although not as often, *The Less Deceived*. On my small bookshelf my fingers scuttle past Frost, Eliot, Pound, Yeats to pluck the thin Larkin volumes almost hidden among them. One has to prepare one's intellect for the great moderns. Often reading Yeats first thing in the morning is like being awakened to the boom of a reverberating gong. Reading Stevens is like having chocolate for breakfast. With Larkin, the tone is matutinal or crepuscular as with most poems, but it is also the tone of ordinary day. His first lines are immediate, and intimate, as if they were resuming an interrupted conversation:

> *Sometimes you hear, fifth-hand,*
> *As epitaph:*
> He chucked up everything
> And just cleared off . . .

—*"Poetry of Departures"*

> *Why should I let the toad* work
>   *Squat on my life?*

—*"Toads"*

No, I have never found
The place where I could say
This is my proper ground,
Here I shall stay . . .

—*"Places, Loved Ones"*

"This was Mr. Bleaney's room . . ."

—*"Mr. Bleaney"*

About twenty years ago
Two girls came in where I worked—
A bosomy English rose
And her friend in specs I could talk to.

—*"Wild Oats"*

When I see a couple of kids
And guess he's fucking her and she's
Taking pills or wearing a diaphragm . . .

—*"High Windows"*

Groping back to bed after a piss . . .

—*"Sad Steps"*

This is not only poetry, it is exchange. No other poet I
know of makes the reader an intimate listener as well as
Larkin does. The poems are not confessional, they are
shared with the reader, with the joke always turning on
Larkin. He would never write:

I have measured out my life in coffee spoons.

The Eliot line is too heraldically plangent. Larkin would describe the spoon. When he eats "an awful pie" at a railway station, the pie is not a symbol—a tacky epiphany. He will continue to eat more pies. "I have measured out my life in awful pies" would be closer to his experience. The railway platforms go on; the awful pies are eaten. The poet does not separate himself from the others in the cheap restaurant. Often the poet, for Larkin, is

> . . . the shit in the shuttered château
> Who does his five hundred words
> Then parts out the rest of the day
> Between bathing and booze and birds . . .

> —"The Life with a Hole in It"

And yet he can startle with this, from "This Be the Verse," the way Marvell suddenly darkens:

> Man hands on misery to man.
>   It deepens like a coastal shelf.
> Get out as early as you can,
>   And don't have any kids yourself.

And, of death:

> Most things may never happen: this one will . . .

> —"Aubade"

:

In verse, tone is one thing, but in pitch lies the seismographic accuracy of the individual voice, the shadings as personal as a thumbprint. Larkin's voice, in the late books *The Whitsun Weddings* and *High Windows*, was accurately set not only in its middle-class timbre but, even more finely, by the use of cliché and aside, and a vocabulary frayed by repetition, perfectly in its milieu, the chat of a librarian or a don, of someone who "also writes verse." The muted pitch is that of a man in a suit, after work, having an ale and a sandwich in a better-than-average pub, as well as that of a guest at an upper-middle-class party, holding a bell-glass of tolerable sherry, nearly dazed with boredom but making small talk. The references in "Naturally the Foundation will Bear Your Expenses" are as swift and compact as shoptalk, and must be difficult not only for some American readers but even for those English readers who may not get the cynical, slightly self-lacerating business of cashing in on the lecture and highbrow radio racket:

> *Hurrying to catch my Comet*
>   *One dark November day,*
> *Which soon would snatch me from it*
>   *To the sunshine of Bombay,*
> *I pondered pages Berkeley*
>   *Not three weeks since had heard,*
> *Perceiving Chatto darkly*
>   *Through the mirror of the Third.*
>
> *Crowds, colourless and careworn,*
>   *Had made my taxi late,*
> *Yet not till I was airborne*
>   *Did I recall the date—*
> *That day when Queen and Minister*
>   *And Band of Guards and all*
> *Still act their solemn-sinister*
>   *Wreath-rubbish in Whitehall.*
>
> *It used to make me throw up,*
>   *These mawkish nursery games:*
> *O when will England grow up?*

—*But I outsoar the Thames,*
And dwindle off down Auster
  To greet Professor Lal
(He once met Morgan Forster),
  My contact and my pal.

The poem's humour lies in its being written, tonally, in dialect; that is, in the argot of chaps who write things, brilliantly mediocre chaps of course, with the conceited casualness of talking only to their peers or compatriots, regardless of whether those outside the circle get the references or not. The poem is set in self-parodic stanzas, again like something from Kipling or a hymn book, making a personal anthem with literature as its subject. And how shockingly accurate it is, precisely because of its pitch! Even a deliberately forced and desperate rhyme like Auster/Forster (simultaneously mocking itself and saying to those outside the circle: "Christ, you know who Auster is, it's the North Wind, for God's sake") pins and immolates the character, an academic ponce.

On the Comet, Britain's pride of the air, he revises a lecture he's given at Berkeley in California (good American bucks for an English accent), then lifts his head from the lecture to look through the jet's window and sees (as through a glass darkly) the publication of the talk by Chatto and Windus over the Third Programme, the English channel devoted to almost nauseating expertise. Then, in the middle stanza, ceremony is mocked. The speaker escapes the grey, self-pumping parade of Remembrance Day, towards the sunshine of India. The smugness of the character is so perfectly adaptable that even the sunshine of Bombay will be exploited, for there he will meet Professor Lal, "my contact and my pal," who once met the author of A *Passage to India*.

But I outsoar the Thames . . .

He's bigger than all that, he's left behind the Thames of Spenser, even of Eliot, the lecture in the briefcase.

And dwindle off down Auster

—the jet is getting smaller and, with it, his sense of responsibility, lost for the career. There is not a more acid portrait of English academic hypocrisy.

Even oral composition is mental writing. Poetry is speech, but it is also writing. Words have shapes. It is composition in verse before it is anything else. Metre precedes breath, shape foreshadows content. Melody indicates meaning. The rest comes afterwards. But in most free verse speech is supposed to shape form.

:

Development, for Larkin, lay not in metrical experiment, or in varieties of stanzaic design, not in Pound's frenzied and very American injunction to "make it new," since Larkin despised the avant-garde, but in concentration on the shifts and pauses possible within the pentameter. Pound had written: "To break the pentameter, that was the first heave," but for Larkin the great achievement was not to betray the pulse or the breath of the pentameter by abandoning it or condemning its melody as archaic, but in exploring the possibility of its defiant consistency, until technical mastery became freshness. The patience and subtlety with which he succeeded in writing "the Larkin line" were not achieved by tricks. There are tricks in modulation as well as tricks of bombast.

Larkin continued to rely on the given beat of the pentametrical line throughout his career. He shadowed it with hesitations, coarsened it with casual expletives, and compacted it with hyphens—when the hyphenated image had always been considered a mark of desperate inertia—to the point where a hyphenated image, with its aural-visual fusion, was powerful enough to contain a minipoem in itself:

Some lonely rain-ceased summer's evening . . .

That vast moth-eaten musical brocade . . .

time's rolling smithy-smoke . . .

dark, shining-leaved cabbages . . .

sun-comprehending glass . . .

Beside grain-scattered streets, barge-crowded water.

The tension of the right-hand margin, the cliff or frontier that the casual, ambulatory breath approached as it neared the edge of the pentameter, pushed description to fall back on the hyphen; but the two paces backwards from the threat of collapse, from the banal enjambment of running the description into an extra half-line and an epigrammatic caesura, was resisted with patient honesty. The compression that ensued out of an absolute devotion to the rhythm produced, in its microcosmic clarity, like a lens or a dew-bead, a world that is whole.

The hyphenated image is not colloquial, but Larkin's achievement is to make it sound as if it were, as if such phrasing could slip into talk, into apparently diffident but actually heraldic observation, as casually as "in a pig's arse, friend." And accepting this, we hear a unified conversational drone, which at the crest of its shared rhythm flashes with illuminating asides, and which flatters us, as Auden often does, into believing that we too are capable of such compressions. After years of sticking to the beat, a devotion that Larkin praised in classic jazz and made him reject Charlie Parker as sneeringly as in painting and in theatre he sneered at Picasso and Beckett, he achieved a clear tone in the instrument, as with the clarinet of Sydney Bechet, while the wire brushes supply the background. The heartbeat is the bass, the wire brushes whir and lift the rhythm, and the improvisations, the stops and rifles of the clear clarinet, may appear to leave the metre, but they return to it, and it is the return that supplies the delight.

II

One of the most flattering experiences I have had was when Larkin included me in his *Oxford Book of Modern Verse* of 1973. I mention this not only from the pride of being recognized by a poet for whose work I had great affection and whose severity of judgement I feared, but also because it contradicts, self-contradicts, the image of a beleaguered provinciality that Larkin offered his readers. This image, continually repeated, was of a weary, sneering recluse who "never read foreign poetry," for whom China was a good place to travel to, if one could get back on the same day, who despised "the myth-kitty" into which poets rummage to pluck classical fragments from the sawdust of the Greco-Roman bran tub, and for whom books were "a load of crap."

Larkin's Oxford anthology, even more eccentric than Yeats's, excluded Commonwealth poets (apart from my own work and that of a couple of others), and to many critics seemed perverse, a papal bull from Hull whose imprimatur sanctified the neglected and minor, giving, for instance, several interminable pages to a poem composed by George Orwell and Alex Comfort. At the expense of Oxford, Larkin seemed to be again taking the mickey out of the literary establishment, to play the conservative when they must have expected daring. By then, however, the Angry Young Men and the red-brick rebels had continued their mugging, like Lucky Jim making faces, until the mugging had reached the rictus of a conservative mask. But we were always that, Kingsley Amis, one of Larkin's close friends, argued, as did John Osborne. What we mocked were the false postures, the old farts' pomposities, the dead mind of Oxbridge. We loved England behind all the face-making and the satire, and the England we loved was one of traditional simplicities. This was the general tone of Larkin's *Oxford Book of English Verse*, which found merit in decently industrious verse, as if its editor were the J. C. Squire of our time. If he found only those values in my own, that was okay by me.

:

Because behind Larkin's cultivated philistinism, one of the penalties of playing the recluse, there was also that perception which, in his own phrase, "loneliness clarifies." But he maintained the mask, physically that of a bespectacled egg-head who was a librarian and hated literature, a waxworks dummy who loved jazz and wrote a column about it for *The Daily Telegraph*, an antipatriot who loved rural England, and who could mock it as he did in "Naturally the Foundation . . ." and still accept a medal from the Queen:

> *That day when Queen and Minister*
> *   And Band of Guards and all*
> *Still act their solemn-sinister*
> *   Wreath-rubbish in Whitehall.*
>
> *It used to make me throw up,*
> *   These mawkish nursery games:*
> *O when will England grow up?*
> *   —But I outsoar the Thames . . .*

But he also wrote the lines that follow, not with the prosaic concern of a conservationist, but with a love as old as Spenser's, and more deeply frightened by highways and "M-1 cafés" than any lines of Betjeman's:

I thought it would last my time—
The sense that, beyond the town,
There would always be fields and farms,
Where the village louts could climb
Such trees as were not cut down;
I knew there'd be false alarms . . .

And that will be England gone,
The shadows, the meadows, the lanes,
The guildhalls, the carved choirs.
There'll be books; it will linger on
In galleries; but all that remains
For us will be concrete and tyres.

—*"Going, Going"*

"And that will be England gone." Who is this? The Rupert Brooke of the Thatcher government celebrating boating, tea, and Granchester? Kipling in the day of the dole? Which Larkin is honest? The one accepting a medal from the very hand it has tried to bite, since there is no real difference between being handed a medal and being draped with a wreath (in fact, some might see both gestures as the handshake of death, as Browning mocked Tennyson for "leaving us for a handful of silver")? Or the other Larkin, the tender elegist pierced by the last light of calendar country? And without irony or ambiguity, the answer is both. Light, with Larkin, is a religious experience. Whether one believes in it or not, as he writes, it goes out, or goes on.

There is an evening coming in
Across the fields, one never seen before,
That lights no lamps.

—*"Going"*

On longer evenings,
Light, chill and yellow,
Bathes the serene
Foreheads of houses.
A thrush sings,
Laurel-surrounded . . .

—"Coming"

If I were called in
To construct a religion
I should make use of water.
. . .
And I should raise in the east
A glass of water
Where any-angled light
Would congregate endlessly.

—"Water"

                    . . . And immediately

Rather than words comes the thought of high windows:
The sun-comprehending glass,
And beyond it, the deep blue air, that shows
Nothing, and is nowhere, and is endless.

—"High Windows"

The tenderness, the prayerlike, sacred translucence of
those lines are in the same spirit as a poem by Edward
Thomas, a spirit that appears fragile because of its precision but that really increases our love for the poet, and
not only for his poetry but for the personality behind the
poetry.

Eliot avoids us, like a man who can't bear being

touched, except by the finger of God. He wrote, with his customary humble vanity, that poetry was a turning away from personality, and that only those who had personality would understand this. That it was not a turning loose of emotion but a turning away from it. By paradox, no poet, if to judge only by features, looks more apersonal than Larkin, and yet few other contemporary poets, even those classified as "confessional," are as intimate and open as that average, antiromantic, bespectacled visage whose personality is stamped on every line, either as observer or as sufferer. We love Larkin, and that is it, simply. And we must be careful to make a distinction between love and popularity. There are minor poets whom we love clearly and cleanly, mainly because they are not posing for their busts. We can discern the edges of hardening marble, the immortalized lineaments when poets turn into bards, can see the seamed toga casually tossed over one shoulder, and eventually we are at a distance from them. As their lines become marmoreal, poets hear their own echo as oracles.

This happened to Eliot with *The Four Quartets*, to Stevens in the plummy vacancies of his later work, to Pound as he began to screech, even to Williams once he felt the laurel tightening on his forehead. Poetry is a narrow spring, the mountain-cold brook of Helicon, and it is not its narrowness that matters but the crystalline, tongue-numbing cold of its freshness, which, in the largest works, still glitters like an unpolluted spring. Larkin is of that stream, and he makes a lot of "great" modern poetry sound like noise. This modesty is saintly, even more than it is hermetic or, amidst the roar and greyness of our cities, reclusive. A great poet like Joyce never lost the narrow, clear, refreshing temperature of that mountain spring, huge as his ambition was, and if there is one great poet who would recognize his kinship with Mr. Bleaney, it would be the one who created Leopold Bloom.

:

I have tried to distinguish love of a poet from his popularity. I would dislike it, for selfish reasons, if Edward Thomas were popular. But I feel happy that Larkin is being so widely read. One of the reasons for his popularity is its accurate placing of the temper of a shrinking Britain. There may even be a general, and even genial, self-mockery in the acceptance of England as tacky and moth-eaten, a place as narrow as its lanes and alleys, jammed with "colourless and careworn" crowds. Larkin's verse is as narrow as this, but it, too, is packed with grey-faced people whose predecessors managed an immense empire.

And, in a sense, Larkin's popularity may be of the same sort as Kipling's, if instead of Victoria we now have Margaret Thatcher. Here he is on the old business of sending troops abroad and having to bring them back:

> *Next year we are to bring the soldiers home*
> *For lack of money, and it is all right.*
> *Places they guarded, or kept orderly,*
> *Must guard themselves, and keep themselves orderly.*
> *We want the money for ourselves at home*
> *Instead of working. And this is all right.*
>
> —*"Homage to a Government"*

—all right, when compared with Kipling's

> *Far called our navies melt away*
> *On dune and headland sinks the fire.*
> *And all our pomp of yesterday*
> *Is one with Nineveh and Tyre . . .*
>
> —*"Recessional"*

Behind Kipling's prophetic posture there is a boast, one that is contained in Byron's "the glory that was Greece / And the grandeur that was Rome." Kipling's High Church lament continues to ascribe glory, even if it will be past, to an empire "once" as great as Nineveh's and Tyre's, the tapestry unfading and hanging in the museum even if the empire has declined. Popular poetry can be excited by sadness, and this is the feeling one gets from hymns, the sweet pain of *sic transit gloria*, because when we as a colonial congregation sang "Recessional," we were sharing the empire's pride in the glory of its passing, like a funeral Viking ship setting out for the horizon, or Arthur's barge in another popular poet of empire, Tennyson.

The opposite is so in Larkin's abrupt, epigrammatic sanity. And yet this has appealed to the very thousands who would have recited Kipling and Tennyson at the peak of the empire's glory and grandeur. If there is one great thing that Larkin's poetry, however temporarily, may have done, it is to make stained glass plain, to clarify, by its transparency, the true ordinariness of post-empire Britain, by supplying his readers with what he calls "a furious, devout drench," without the twilight trumpets and the doom.

> Next year we shall be living in a country
> That brought its soldiers home for lack of money.
> The statues will be standing in the same
> Tree-muffled squares, and look nearly the same.
> Our children will not know it's a different country.
> All we can hope to leave them now is money.

—*"Homage to a Government"*

:

Larkin's is a poetry of clichés. But the clichés inspire him to pursue them carefully towards some cryptic or sometimes illuminating resolution. Bleaney alone in his room;

an admirer turning the pages of a photograph album; spring in the park with its prams and nurses; sticking to one's job while daydreaming of adventure; parking a bicycle outside a church and removing cycle clips; trains, windows, streets. It is like LaForgue, in its urban geography, its elegiac domesticity, the sadness of the professional traveller encountering the glitter of set cutlery in provincial hotels, and clichés need a language of cliché.

Herein lies Larkin's astounding courage. Poets with similar themes, like MacNeice, or the early Eliot and the early Auden, wrote of cities and isolation, but never that relentlessly, never with the varied repetitiveness that Larkin takes to be the metre of life.

To reinforce his craft he chose models whose subjects were first of all ordinary, banal: Betjeman, the novelist Barbara Pym, Stevie Smith. The process of the spirit was through the rubbed, worn-out familiarity of the common to something that would shine from that friction, as it does at the end of "The Whitsun Weddings":

> . . . *and what it held*
> *Stood ready to be loosed with all the power*
> *That being changed can give. We slowed again,*
> *And as the tightened brakes took hold, there swelled*
> *A sense of falling, like an arrow-shower*
> *Sent out of sight, somewhere becoming rain.*

and in the blazing epiphany at the end of his celebration of some imaginary minor master, with its wonderful, leaping assonances of crusted logs aflame and the hiss of spit into the flames in "The Card-Players":

> *Rain, wind and fire! The secret, bestial peace!*

Once, the delight was underlined by the fact that there was so little of Larkin's poetry, that its scale refreshed its rarity, and that what little there was was perfect, so useful and private that the poems felt as familiar as a bunch of keys. One picked them up as casually; they were small, shining, and slipped easily into the pocket of memory. Now, of course, another Larkin joke has been played on us. *The Collected Poems* is not an immense block of a book, but it is large, containing several dozen previously unpublished poems, and its very prolixity is a contradiction of the parsimonious writer we believed Larkin to be. He said late in his life that he had not abandoned poetry but that it had abandoned him. We waited for years for the next Larkin poem, patient, because we anticipated its metrical perfection. In the meantime, we could always go back to those volumes we were beginning to know by heart from rereading. Now this proof of Larkin as a fecund, if not voluminous, poet is both startling and amusing. It means that he once wrote as hard and as often as any other poet of his time, and how does the ample Larkin compare with the almost anorexic slenderness of his last book, *High Windows*?

There aren't any juvenilia in Anthony Thwaite's collection. The book is not stuffed with negligible, purely biographical poems that might show us Larkin's development. Instead, the verse is, in Larkin's own phrase, "nutritious," the skill unfaltering even in apprenticeship. The thin Larkin managed to get out of the fat one mainly because of the severity of his judgement, even if all the poems in the collected volume were publishable, and it makes us admire him even more that he could have found so many excellent poems unsatisfactory enough to have kept them from print. The choices had nothing to do with career or with being a perfectionist. What it had to do with was his belief in breathing, in the poem's life. Thus the lovely poems that he remarkably excluded from his narrow books fail only in the sense that they best belong not to his reputation but to poetry. Larkin is a moral poet, an honest one, who hated grandeur and the posing that encourages experiment. This is not conservatism; it is, purely, devotion. And this is why poets will continue to cherish him beyond his current popularity—for that crisp dismissal of "what's not good enough," or what "has nothing to say," which, if applied to so many of his contemporaries, would reduce them to a few lines of poetry, enough, in his view, for any lifetime.

The text has its chronological delights. An early poem (1943–44), "Dawn," printed in full below:

> To wake, and hear a cock
> Out of the distance crying,
> To pull the curtains back
> And see the clouds flying—
> How strange it is
> For the heart to be loveless, and as cold as these.

will be rewritten twenty-four years later as:

> Groping back to bed after a piss
> I part thick curtains, and am startled by
> The rapid clouds, the moon's cleanliness.
>
> Four o'clock: wedge-shadowed gardens lie
> Under a cavernous, a wind-picked sky.
> There's something laughable about this,
>
> The way the moon dashes through clouds that blow
> Loosely as cannon-smoke to stand apart
> (Stone-coloured light sharpening the roofs below)

which develops a voracity for accurate passion:

High and preposterous and separate—
Lozenge of love! Medallion of art!
O wolves of memory! Immensements! No,

One shivers slightly, looking up there.

—*"Sad Steps,"* 1968

and the Chekhovian, plucked string of:

I listen to money singing. It's like looking down
From long french windows at a provincial town,
The slums, the canal, the churches ornate and mad
In the evening sun. It is intensely sad.

—*"Money,"* 1973

True. Except that his sadness is now our delight.

(1989)

Ted Hughes

Ted Hughes's reputation may be enduring an eclipse of fashion because the preference now is for a verse that is detailed, actual, for elegiac sociology, the ordinary ordinarily recorded. His poetry is lonely and remote. Towers and hieratic stones are out of fashion; mist and ragged moors, Hardyesque stoicism seem far too fabulous for contemporary verse's long season of common sense and urban light. Its mineral strength is condemned or ignored as a posturing, but one might as well accuse Stonehenge of having a stance.

The poetry is surveyed as a tour of primordial ruins, but the power of Hughes's work is that it preserves its own archaicness, that it shows us an England besieged by a rising sea of trash. It sometimes snarls back at us like a hounded, embayed beast, cornered and bleeding. Its width is massive, its ecology desperate.

Nature, in English poetry before Hughes, was a decent panacea. One went towards it, entered it like a roofless cathedral. It was a place of contemplation, not terror. It was the benign shrine of the pathetic fallacy. Sheep might softly graze there without blood and droppings. It often went no deeper than the surface of a shiny calendar, or the tender pieties of a child's book. Preceding Hughes, Lawrence demythologized all this. The myth of the Sabine farm with the farm shit, the deaths and squealings that nobody wants to hear about or hear, Blake's little lamb strangled in a birth caul.

But if Hughes's poetry were simply a matter of antithesis to pastoral, of showing the scabs and welts, the wounds of a long-suffering but enduring landscape without figures, without the Wordsworthian narcissism of contemplating imagination by its reflection in lakes made sacred by piety, then the pitch of his natural observations would be simply that of a school bully dangling a dead frog in the reader's face. And that is what they think: those who turn away from the page as a girl might from a dead frog.

Well, it was about time that a language which did not distance itself from nature by botanical pastoral catalogues thrust its vision through a cloud of flies and examined carcasses with the disturbing casualness, the long, guttural offhand phrases in Hughes's rhythm, of an abrupt farmer. Because the carcase was English poetry as well, not only that of a rotting sheep.

An interior decay may still be gnawing away at that carcase, and if Hughes's vision may be the bones of that poetry picked clean by crows, of bare ridges with a few memorial rocks, then it only carries, in its wide-ranging view, not apocalyptic fury, not a rage to frighten, but that barrenness that is there in the great Hebrew poets, Isaiah, Jeremiah, Job—the bare Yorkshire moors in stony light. Because the earth is going. Its topsoil is spinning away in dust. Because the sea is foul. Because the air is poison. Because the streams are sick.

But this is not the poetry of our day-to-day lives. These truths are too big and we believe they will go away if we concentrate on small, consoling things. So, naturally, we wish Hughes would go away. We wish he'd go and keep on practising to be a monolith. A monodic monolith. We can't stand his tone.

Hughes brought to poetry a toughness that was unbearable, a medusa-face that paralyzed the high chatter that passes for criticism of the craft. In Sylvia Plath the toughness cracks apart into a hysteria that is almost clinical. Once the poetry of breakdown became popular, Hughes's had to become increasingly passé, because its strength was not personal, and therefore its endurance seemed pitiless and cruel. Yet the difference between Hughes and a poet like Robinson Jeffers, or even Lawrence, is that he does not carve his own visage from stone.

There isn't any Ted Hughes in Hughes's poetry of landscape. The "I," when it is there, is not taller than its surroundings. He is a poet of terror, not of the insomniac terrors of Plath, the muse of aspirin, but in the immense sense of terror, the Greek example of awe. The tragedy of white stones, not white pills, of the sudden asterisk of blood on the stones, of what Auden calls "libation and sacrifice." Would that it were all an act! But the mask is in the face. They say of marriage that man and wife eventually resemble each other. Poets come to look like their poetry. The page is a mirror, a pool. Hughes's face emerges through the pane of paper in its weathered openness as both friendly and honest. It speaks trust. The way a stone appears to speak about itself.

It is time to give up the image of the old blood-and-guts Hughes, the Patton of modern poetry, the bayed wolf always and only snarling back from its corner of England, and time to be touched by the tenderness it conceals behind the furious vocabulary, because it is a precious and common tenderness, as wet-eyed as the eternal dewiness of Edward Thomas's vision. Its rage is concern, not a prehistoric, macho blustering, and its genius is feminine, that of the female we call Mother Earth.

That exterior roughage, that nap of the furred hide rubbed backwards, not letting the line be smoothed and petted by our agreeing, that condition of always being rubbed the wrong way, isn't the same as saying that every panther is a pussycat at heart, and yet in its eyes there is a mortal tenderness. That is wolf-watching. That is the *sunt lacrimae rerum* that glitters in the eyes even of beasts. Our own eyes are harder than those of the beasts. We are the real predators:

> *For this is the Black Rhino, who vanishes as he approaches*
> *Every second there is less and less of him*
> *By the time he reaches you nothing will remain, maybe, but*
> *   the horn . . .*

The poem is itself predatory. It eats its subject, and the beautiful and terrifying honesty of Hughes's poetry is that it does not distance our ambiguity through moral outrage. Every poem of Hughes is its own elegy, yet the tone is never simply elegiac, never "If I should die" or "When I have fears that I may cease to be"; its brutal ecology is that even the most sensitive "I" degenerates into biodegradable rubbish; that even poetry, along with the rhino, is continually threatened with extinction. His "Thrushes" are fierce, stabbing machines, not by his own antithesis, but by nature's. But they are beautiful, and the poem that closes in on their beaks becomes clear and beautiful because there is no such thing as irony in nature.

The poetry of Hughes has brought us, in the most exact sense, closer to nature, its complete workings, than any English poet we can think of, including Clare and Hardy. Not because it is brutal, but because it is brutal and bright; otherwise all we would have would be a morose accuracy, the diary of a depressed naturalist. It is a poetry of exultation. It is behind its threshing furore as quiet as his "Dove":

Now staying
Coiled on a bough
Bubbling molten, wobbling top-heavy
Into one and many.

Also this:

Slips from your eye-corner-overtaking
Your first thought.
Through your mulling gaze over haphazard earth.
Laser the lark-shaped hole
In the lark's song.

Hughes's metre, for all the length of its lines, is not really Lawrentian or Whitmanesque, by which is usually meant that it is delivered from formal constraints, expansive and recent; instead, it is ancestral, rooted in Middle English, its phrases divided by a heavy caesura that often has the depth of a geological fissure, an abyss into which we are afraid to look.

The heredity in Hughes's metre requires considerable devotion to poetry. The history of it works the field with the rigour and metre of ancient tillage. It works it in the ugliest weather, and even though it may upheave and charge through our ideas of pastoral with the blunt power of a tractor, behind its belligerent growl there is a distant, older rhythm of poetry as work that goes as far back and as deep as Langland.

What else could it celebrate but force? What else can it believe in but an endurance beyond itself, and without the tiring buoyancy of Whitman, the moral evangelism of Lawrence, the modest botany of the Georgians? It seems to long for the whirlwind of anonymity, for the cold severity of pebbles as primal nouns. For terror, but for the terror of the great Greek tragic-poets. The moors revert to arenas of sacrifice. The gods are bloodied figures. The cheapest evasion is to call this myth-making.

Sometimes to read a Hughes poem is like trying to go out in bad weather, unaccommodated. The alternative is comfortable. To sit indoors and sip poems written for indoors. But great tragic poets require moral bravery from us, and that ancient virtue, of responsibility as awe, appears to be threatened with extinction like everything else. We do not want to hear this. We leave prophets to their job of prophesying, and prefer the domesticated, consoling mutter of contemporary verse, the metre of decent conversation, believing that poetry, as prophesy, is part of a very distant past. Often the stony light of Hughes's poetry seems to come as far back as the primal, tribal dawn of England.

It has a hallowing width, a spreading power, a tireless compassion like sunrise. It is Caedmon with old car tyres and cold tractors in the morning. It shakes us awake and we read it for what it is, hard work. Its weather comes off the cold page with bracing, exhilarating realness. It is to be cherished any way we like, but, most naturally, with that irascible affection the English have always had for their climate.

It is, in every phrase, as pious as a bead of dew or the droppings of a sheep. It is so in Hughes's eyes, bless them.

> *Take telegraph wires, a lonely moor,*
> *And fit them together. The thing comes alive in your ear.*
> *Towns whisper to towns over the heather . . .*

and not his eyes only, but bless the pricked, sharp attention of his world-watching ears.

(1989)

Crocodile Dandy:

Les Murray

The barbarians approaching the capital bring with them
not only the baggage of a cow-horned, shaggy army but
also the vandalization of the imperial language. They bring
their bards with them, as well as their camp followers.
What is repulsive about these bards, however, is not that
they elevate the dialect of the tribe (that is to be expected)
but that they can recite long passages of the imperial literature as if it were their own; and with a vigour, even a
love, that brings a blush to the civilized cheek. They come
over the line of the sands with lances and camels, but also
with the cacophony of the pots and pans of a dented provincial vocabulary. Therefore the defenders invite the
bards to dinner. They drape their hairy shoulders with the
sashes of the Academy. They are fascinated by the burrs
and thistles of their accents, while remaining astounded
by their scholarship. But the temples are not threatened,
the city is intact, because the barbarians have the same
table manners, and have every intention of returning
home.

Let the shaggy, long horde of spiky letters and the
dark rumbling of hexametrical phalanxes rise over the outback towards the capital of the English language, and you

have, like a scene out of a Mad Max movie, something of the shaggy power, grace, and mass of Les Murray's poems. They quake on the page. They leave tracks like home-built engines. They stagger and they are staggering. They can be walked around like eccentric but practical inventions, but only Mr. Murray knows how to drive them.

You can call him Les. I assure you that he would not mind. This custom of the barbarians, this habit of calling new and presumably cursory acquaintances by their first names from the second sentence, makes the capital wince. This is still how one distinguishes Americans from Englishmen, and this formality, this courtesy of advancing politely in squares, a strategy little different from shaking hands and nodding, may have something to do with losing the Revolutionary War. It certainly attracts Australians to Americans. Perhaps the barbarians cannot manage the third person. One is at a loss to know why. Or it may have to do with a sense of space; for somehow, the wider the geography, the terser the vocabulary; whether it be the monosyllables of sailors, cowboys, or pioneers of the outback. Although this seems to be turning Murray into the appointed bard of the Australian wastes, a kind of Crocodile Dandy, the joy is that the poems of his two volumes printed in this country, *The Vernacular Republic* and *The Daylight Moon*, have a width and an affability that may sound garrulous by contrast with the myth of the terse pioneer, though they have the same accent, the same tonal truth.

Connect this shambling off of the third person in grammar with the shrug that accommodates history, that refuses to treat it as noble but neutered, but rather as a bit of a shambles through which one walks in khaki shorts, and you will get closer to Les than you might to Mr. Murray. In fact, he has a poem about shorts. It is called "The Dream of Wearing Shorts Forever," a longish poem that ends

. . . walking meditatively
among green timber, through the grassy forest
towards a calm sea
and looking across to more of that great island
and the further topics.

Reader, this does not mean that you can put your arm around him or, for that matter, encircle his imagination, because Murray is a very large man with a very large mind. What it does mean is that you can get into the verse immediately, as you can with Kipling. (The dead need no formal introductions.) His range is history, and our sense of his scholarship vital and immense. All the barbarians have traditional antecedents; but he makes sure that breadth is its beginning, that his invitation to enter a vernacular republic is not a hearty, beer-lifting "Welcome to Osstrailya" but as open an invitation to the soul to feel the freshness of any part of the world, from Sydney to the ruins of Rome, as Whitman's horizon-wide title, "Leaves of Grass."

The language of grass is the vernacular republic, the phenomenon (and the contradiction) of a daylight moon powerful in its persistence, elate in its indifference to digital time. These are not words to Murray: soul, love, humanity. They are not believed in with a parsonical vigour. They are natural, they are fated, they are what we are. *The Daylight Moon* is dedicated to the glory of God. The last time that a bard wrote such a birthday card to the Almighty, apart from Dylan Thomas's dedication of his *Collected Poems*, it was probably a monk, not an ascetic one, but a wandering wide-eyed friar, a Franciscan. There is no poetry in the English language now so rooted in its sacredness, so broad-leafed in its pleasures, and yet so intimate and so conversational:

It's our annual visit to the latitudes
of rice, kerosene and resignation . . .

. . .

an intrusive, heart-narrowing season
at this far southern foot of the monsoon.
As the kleenex flower, the hibiscus
drops its browning wads, we forget
annually, as one forgets a sickness.
The stifling days will never come again,
not now that we've seen the first sweater
tugged down on the beauties of division
and inside the rain's millions, a risen
loaf of cat on a cool night verandah.

—*"A Retrospect of Humidity"*

Or:

. . . listen for black Freudian beaches; they seek a miles-wide
    pustular
rock dome of pure Crude, a St. Paul's-in-profundis. There
    are many
wrong numbers on the geophone, but it's brought us some
    distance, and by car.
Every machine has been love and a true answer.

—*"Machine Portraits with Pendant Spaceman"*

There is a difference between vigour and energy. Vigour can be the imagination lifting weights. Energy is the magic that levitates objects. Kipling was vigorous, Hopkins was energetic. What is called "noise" in poetry occurs when even a poet as great as Yeats attempts to elevate vigour into energy. (He himself wrote that "out of the quarrel with others we make rhetoric, out of the quarrel with ourselves we make poetry.") It is vigour that makes so much of "The Wreck of the Deutschland" noisy, so unlike Hopkins's religious sonnets. The difference between vigour and energy is, quite simply, the difference between Emily Dickinson and Walt Whitman. Dickinson has so much energy that she can afford to be narrow, but Whitman's vigorous and hearty exhortations can tire, like a camp counsellor urging all us tired boys to come down to the old Indian lake, when we'd rather sit here considering one of Miss Dickinson's worms or sparrows. It is also, to batter the point, one of the reasons why, in this age of muttering soliloquies, of mildly tormented asides, an energy like Ted Hughes is misjudged as being a "noisy" poet. Noise is an attribute of praise. "Make a joyful noise unto the Lord, all ye lands." But contemporary verse, in its modest self-centredness, its muted, agnostic shit-kicking, averts its face from awe.

   :

There is Beerbohm's famous cartoon of Whitman inviting the American eagle to soar in front of a dour and sceptical Queen Victoria. Les Murray's position now in Australian literature takes that risk. But he knows that to become the bard of modern Australia, to celebrate its spaces and its convict past, is only to make a predictable noise. A patriotic flapping. But the power, and the persistence, of his celebration is religious, and without assaulting us, because he is doing something so ordinary, so vernacular, and yet so fated, that it must make criticism cower; it is making poetry holy.

A man who has known deserts believes in wells. We turn our wells on through faucets, and by commonness and familiarity we diminish the elemental sacredness of water. If Murray's poetry gushes, then bless it, because it is the gushing not of an oil strike or of a convivial, "matey" garrulity, but of the striking by a rod in the desert. It cannot help its force:

> Dream surrounds, is infused with this world. It is not
> subordinate.
> We come from it; we live at tangents and accords with it;
> we go
> back into it, at last, through the drowsing torture chambers
> to it.
>
> We have gills for dream-life, in our head; we must keep them
> wet
> from the nine-nights' immense, or dreams will emerge bodily,
> and enforce it.
> Hide among or deny the shallow dreadful ones, and they may
> stay out . . .

—"The Dialect of Dreams"

It would also have been easier for Murray to be hermetic, to moor himself out in some enthusiastic wasteland on his subcontinent, away from machines and the corruptions of civilization, to play the applaudable part of a white aborigine, delving in myth for material. But the poems praise technology not as a marvel, of course, but as part of the growth of human nature, secondary and functional. And they celebrate these engines, not from a distance, like Whitman's "To a Locomotive," admiring their lines and power as if they were arranged in an exhibition, but as working things, things we enter and use. Expressionist poetry of the early Russian Revolution in which machines are praised is no different from pre-Raphaelitism. An object is idealized into a glow through an amber filter, a powerful tenderness. Vigour is again confused with energy. The enthusiasm of Kipling for machines, in a poem like "MacAndrew's Hymn," is political in intention; it is on the same level as O'Neill's *The Hairy Ape*, in which the worker with the oilcloth and the sacred stains on his face becomes superior to the class for whose safety he is responsible. The joy in Murray, however, is that he is the engineer:

> And entering on the only smooth road
> this steamer glides past the rattling shipyard
> where they're having the usual Aboriginal
> whale-feast in reverse, with scaffolding and planking;
> engine smoke marching through blue sheoak trees
> along the edge of Jack Robertson farms,
> the river opens and continually opens
>
> and lashed on deck, a Vauxhall car,
> intricate in brass, with bonnet grooves,
> a bulb to squawk, great guillotine levers,
> high diamond-buttoned leather club chairs
> and dressing-table windscreen to flash afar:
> in British cherry metal, detailed in mustard
> it cruises up country with a moveless wheel.

—*"Federation Style on the Northern Rivers"*

If, in poems less calm and measured than the one quoted above, Murray's metre sometimes achieves the monody of a piston, instead of a heartbeat, it has a lot to do with scale, with the imperative of expansion. But sometimes Murray pummels you with the resources of a vocabulary so jaunty in its confidence that it becomes truly jingoistic in its belligerence, insisting that one had better learn his language if one is going to travel the wide map of the verse, and in his own accent, at that:

Mr Nouveau Jack old man my legs are all paralysed up.
Black smuts swirled weightless in the room
   some good kind person
like the nausea of the novice free-falling in a
   deep mine's cage . . .

—*"Letters to the Winner"*

It is not that the vocabulary is different. The italicized words are from a letter, and the other words are English, and not Australian English particularly. The rush and sputter of the line, the packed half-puns and off-rhymes, are like technical fireworks, and their succession of explosions can only be managed exactly by imagining Murray's own voice. Every poet of achievement writes with his own voice, finally, even his own accent, inflection, tone, though the posture is sometimes too burly.

There is a difference, however, between entering the tone and mimicking it, because such mimicry only creates difference, or even indifference, like a challenge we do not want to take on. Carried to the point of resistance, it is this, of course, that irritates or frightens the defenders of the capital language: they are quite willing to admit Australian into English, but they have no intention of repeating it in the very melody on which it is based. The gates will yield, and the language will be expanded, even wider than the physical borders of the empire. The language of the former provinces and protectorates and dominions must beware, however, of another kind of arrogance, of a sort of vernacular or sublime revenge, or, less vehemently, of a challenge. Only big poets can be parodied; and it is one of the signs of a major poet that Murray comes close to self-parody.

Murray's tone is vernacular, but not his vocabulary. He has not devised, like Whitman, a metre that is consistent, as open to adaptation as that of the Old Testament poets, a rhythm that is both prophesy and bequest. Whitman proclaims a new form, a new breadth for his new country, in a line as long as its new horizons, opening up poetry in the same way that his pioneers were opening up America. But broad as this poetry appeared to be, it also had, at its centre, a narrow didactic passion, a presumption of inevitability in its evangelism, its proclamations that for American poets this was the only way to see and therefore to write.

Whitman's heirs have continued in that voice, the voice of the didact, the voice of vigour opposed to the claim of energy. Modern American poetics is as full of its sidewalk hawkers as a modern American city: *this* is the only metre, *this* is the American way to breathe, *this* is the variable foot. One can stop and watch the cup-and-bean demonstrations from Pound, to Williams, to Ginsberg, to Duncan, to Oppen, challenging young American bystanders to try it, then pass on, shaking one's head at how shrill some of Walt's boys have become.

I do not mean this aside to assault the tiring, variable pamphlets forced into those very old cultures that Whitman urged his boys to erase as overpaid accounts. To stand between Kipling and Whitman must have meant some confusion. To avoid the elegiac Kipling of the empire's sunset, as well as the oracular sunrise of the new world (American Australia); to resist the evangelism of proclaiming that there was something called Australian foot; to learn to deafen himself to all the booths of the poetics bazaar, some howling, some with the soft monosyllabic sell, meant that Murray had to wait for the proper light to fall across his mind and his page, a light untinted and unfiltered through patriotism or guilt. And the light had to be ordinary: daylight, Australian day.

This is the light that comes off the pages of *The Vernacular Republic* and *The Daylight Moon*, the hard light of ordinariness, almost a glare. Murray is not an elegiac poet, which again could have been a great career move. Instead, he has manufactured a syntax that digests iron and spits out petals. If he is anything, he is Roman in the way that Ben Jonson was Roman, firm-based and pillared with scholarship, way above the tiny hawkers below in the market. Not many daylight moons ago, the barbarians were admired from a distance for certain things peculiar to them—a rough charm, a vigour, an enthusiasm that permitted them to do their unabashed bellowing to God on behalf of the capital named Literature—of which the dandies and the eunuchs of the empire are no longer capable. It is easy to hear any one of those voices urging Murray to keep his voice down. But here we have a poet whose open duty, and he proclaims it repeatedly (tiringly, if you like), is praise. A poet who has himself been praised, but who would, to the amazement of his adulators, rather go home, put on his khaki shorts, and write like this:

> *Sprawl is really classless, though. It's John Christopher*
>   *Frederick Murray*
> *asleep in his neighbours' best bed in spurs and oilskins*
> *but not having thrown up:*
> *sprawl is never Calum who, drunk, along the hallways of*
>   *our house,*
> *reinvented the Festoon. Rather*
> *it's Beatrice Miles going twelve hundred ditto in a taxi,*
> *No Lewd Advances, No Hitting Animals, No Speeding,*
> *on the proceeds of her two-bob-a-sonnet Shakespeare*
>   *readings.*
> *An image of my country. And would that it were more so.*

> —*"The Quality of Sprawl"*

but like this as well:

> *Those hills are ancient stone gods*
> *just beginning to be literature.*

—*"Flood Plains on the Coast Facing Asia"*

(*1989*)

The Road Taken:
Robert Frost

On that gusting day of the inauguration of the young emperor, the sublime Augustan moment of a country that was not just a republic but also an empire, no more a home-spun vision of pioneer values but a world power, no figure was more suited to the ceremony than Robert Frost. He had composed a poem for the occasion, but he could not read it in the glare and the wind, so instead he recited one that many had heard and perhaps learned by heart.

> *The land was ours before we were the land's.*
> *She was our land more than a hundred years*
> *Before we were her people.*

This was the calm reassurance of American destiny that provoked Tonto's response to the Lone Ranger. No slavery, no colonization of Native Americans, a process of dispossession and then possession, but nothing about the dispossession of others that this destiny demanded. The choice of poem was not visionary so much as defensive. A Navajo hymn might have been more appropriate: the "ours" and the "we" of Frost were not as ample and multi-hued as Whitman's tapestry, but something as tight and regional as a Grandma Moses painting, a Currier and Ives print, strictly New England in black and white.

By then as much an emblem of the republic as any rubicund senator with his flying white hair, an endangered species like a rare owl, there was the old poet who, between managing the fluttering white hair and the fluttering white paper, had to recite what sounded more like an elegy than a benediction. "The land was ours before we were the land's" could have had no other name, not only because he was then in his old age, but because all his spirit and career, like Thomas Hardy's, lurched toward a wintry wisdom.

:

Robert Frost: the icon of Yankee values, the smell of wood smoke, the sparkle of dew, the reality of farmhouse dung, the jocular honesty of an uncle.

Why is the favorite figure of American patriotism not paternal but avuncular? Because uncles are wiser than fathers. They have humor, they keep their distance, they are bachelors, they can't be fooled by rhetoric. Frost loved playing the uncle, relishing the dry enchantment of his own voice, the homely gravel in the throat, the keep-your-distance pseudo-rusticity that suspected every stranger, meaning every reader. The voice is like its weather. It tells you to stay away until you are invited. Its first lines, in the epigraph to Frost's 1949 *Complete Poems*, are not so much invitations as warnings.

> *I'm going out to clean the pasture spring;*
> *I'll only stop to rake the leaves away*
> *(And wait to watch the water clear, I may):*
> *I sha'n't be gone long.—You come too.*

From the very epigraph, then, the surly ambiguities slide in. Why "I may"? Not for the rhyme, the desperation of doggerel, but because of this truth: that it would take too long to watch the agitated clouded water settle, that is, for as long as patience allows the poet to proceed to the next line. (Note that the parentheses function as a kind of container, or bank, or vessel, of the churned spring.) The refrain, "You come too." An invitation? An order? And how sincere is either? That is the point of Frost's tone, the authoritative but ambiguous distance of a master ironist.

Frost is an autocratic poet rather than a democratic poet. His invitations are close-lipped, wry, quiet; neither the voice nor the metrical line has the open-armed municipal mural expansion of the other democratic poet, Whitman. The people in Frost's dramas occupy a tight and taciturn locale. They are not part of Whitman's parade of blacksmiths, wheelwrights made communal by work. Besieged and threatened, their virtues are as cautious and measured as the scansion by which they are portrayed.

Many of the uncollected poems in the Library of America's *Robert Frost: Collected Poems, Prose, and Plays* are negligible, but only because they pale beside the triumph of the best and familiar Frost. They neither add to nor detract from the reputation. There is a hefty representation of them, and like all the famous whose every fragment is hoarded by the academy, Frost has to pay for his fame with certain embarrassments, such as this verse from 1890:

> *The 'tzin quick springeth to his side,*
> *His mace he hurls on high,*
> *It crasheth through the Spanish steel,*
> *And Leon prone doth lie.*

and:

> *When I was young, we dwelt in a vale*
> *By a misty fen that rang all night,*
> *And thus it was the maidens pale . . .*

Through the Wordsworthian vocabulary of "Upon each grove and mead," to the ambulatory reflection on the pastoral sublime, the evolving Frost is predictable, dutiful as the early Keats is to Milton, to what is expected of the nature poet. First, there is the generic blur, and then, as in John Clare, the haze lifts and leaf and stone are magnified in detail like grass after a rain shower. We rattle the box for gems among the dud stones and find "Genealogical" and "The Middletown Murder" and this early one (c. 1890s) which is equal in steadiness to middle Frost:

> The reason of my perfect ease
> In the society of trees
> Is that their cruel struggles pass
> Too far below my social class
> For me to share them or be made
> For what I am and love afraid.

And there is the early debt to Hardy:

> Those stones out under the low-limbed tree
> Doubtless bear names that the mosses mar.

:

By technical convention and even in tone, the poet of *A Boy's Will* is an English poet, not a New England poet, an exiled Georgian, already skillful in the springing resilience of his verses and the measured plot of harmony and homily in their stanzas. There are signs of that cunning of adaptation, of seizure, that great poets show in their ambition, the way Eliot shamelessly raided Laforgue; and so we can watch Frost stalking Hardy through shadowy woods, keeping his own distance, but measuring his own hesitancy until he takes his own road, which will diverge from Hardy and the English pastoralists, and hits his own stride, this jocular stride of the open road apparent in W. H. Davies, in Whitman, in "Two Tramps in Mud Time."

In 1912, when he was thirty-eight, Frost left Boston with his family for England, to devote himself to writing. He submitted *A Boy's Will*, his first collection, to the English publisher David Nutt, and it was accepted. He lived in a cottage in Buckinghamshire. In London, at Harold Munro's Poetry Bookshop, he met the poet F. S. Flint, who introduced him to Ezra Pound. Pound gave *A Boy's Will* a good review because, for all his aggressive cosmopolitanism and campaigning for the classics and "the new," Pound was as much a vernacular regional poet as Frost, and the genuine Americanness of Frost must have stirred a patriotic claim in him as much as the tonal authenticity of Eliot did. He derided the falsely modern and saw a classic shape in Frost that made "it" (poetry) new by its directness and its vigor: Frost's writing achieved a vernacular elation in tone, not with the cheap device of dialect spelling or rustic vocabulary, but with a clean ear and a fresh eye. (Pound found the same qualities in Hemingway.) And Yeats told Pound that *A Boy's Will* was "the best poetry written in America for a long time." The judgment remains right.

It was in England, in discussions with Flint and T. E. Hulme, that Frost clarified his direction by "the sounds of sense with all their irregularity of accent across the regular beat of the metre." Pound's encouragement—or, better, his papal benediction—turned into belligerence. Frost calls Pound a "quasi-friend" and writes: "He says I must write something much more like *vers libre* or he will let me perish by neglect. He really threatens." He worries that Pound's good review of *North of Boston* will describe him as one of Pound's "party of American literary refugees." (Later, down the years, down their different roads, Frost petitioned against Pound's imprisonment, even if he was enraged at the award of the Bollingen Prize to him; and Pound himself had no choice but to recognize the syntactical variety in Frost's verse, the *vers libre* within the taut frame.)

:

Frost's early mastery of stress looks natural. A deftness, like a skipping stone, evades the predictable scansion by a sudden parenthesis, by a momentarily forgotten verb— "that laid the swale in rows . . . and scared a bright green snake," and shifting, dancing caesuras.

> *Anything more than the truth would have seemed too weak*
> *To the earnest love that laid the swale in rows,*
> *Not without feeble-pointed spikes of flowers*
> *(Pale orchises), and scared a bright green snake.*

Yet the dialogue of the dramatic poems is boxed in by a metrical rigidity that, strangely enough, is more stiff-backed than the narration, perhaps because these poems are thought of as one element of the whole poem rather than as theater, where narration recedes in the presence of action and the variety of individual voices solidifies the contradictions of melody character by character. "The Death of the Hired Man" and others are poems, and not plays, for this reason: the voice of the characters and their creator is one voice, Frost's, and one tone, something nearer to complaint and elegy than vocal conflict, the tragic edge instead of tragedy. It's as if all his characters were remembering poems by Robert Frost. From "A Hundred Collars":

> *"It's business, but I can't say it's not fun.*
> *What I like best's the lay of different farms,*
> *Coming out on them from a stretch of woods,*
> *Or over a hill or round a sudden corner.*
> *I like to find folks getting out in spring.*
> *Raking the dooryard, working near the house."*

:

A certain deadening of the ear had dated dramatic verse since the Victorians, who tried to resuscitate Elizabethan and Jacobean drama through the pentameter, prolonging a hollow, martial echo that could not render the ordinary and domestic, that did not take into account the charged and broken syntax of Webster or the late Shakespeare. The same reverential monody occurred in Victorian epic poetry. The Elizabethan echo had become part of the soaring architecture, a determination to be sublime that again divided the lyric from the dramatic voice, that took poetry away from the theatre and back into the library. Frost felt that in New England he was being offered an unexplored, unuttered theatre, away from the leaves of libraries, in a natural setting rich with stories and characters.

We think of Frost's work in theatrical terms, with the poet, of course, as its central character, mocking his crises, his stopping at a crossroads, but also because of the voices in the poems. These voices are American, but their metre is not as subtly varied as the lyrical and yet colloquial power of his own meditations. To read the "Masques," at least for this reader, is a duty, not a delight. One keeps wishing that they were plays, not theatrical poems. The vocabulary grows ornate:

> The myrrh tree gives it. Smell the rosin burning?
> The ornaments the Greek artificers
> Made for the Emperor Alexius . . .
> . . .
> And hark, the gold enameled nightingales
> Are singing.

The line is sometimes unspeakable:

> You poor, poor swallowable little man.

The humour is arch:

Job: But, yes, I'm fine, except for now and then
A reminiscent twinge of rheumatism.

"Vulgarity," the gift that comes from the mob, which great poetic dramatists possess, no matter how sublime their rhetoric, and which they need in order to force a single response from an audience, springs from the vernacular, from the oral rather than the written, and is based on popular banalities of humour and pathos—this power is what separates, say, Browning from Shakespeare, this eagerness to entertain, to put it crassly. With his own gifts of the vernacular and of self-dramatization, Frost might be expected to have produced a wide, popular theatre, since the tone of American speech was ready and resolved. And yet, for all his winking and his intimacy, Frost is a very private poet.

When we imagine the single voice of Frost behind the lines, it is the sound of a personal vernacular, but heard as dialogue. The vernacular petrifies into the monodic, perhaps because the dramatic poem (is there a single really successful example in literature?) is a kind of mule, like the prose poem, and like the "Masques." The contradiction of any masque is the pitch of its diction; it is meant not to be acted but to be heard. Frost's theatrical dialogue has a monodic drone. Yeats, who in the beginning of his theatrical career was as dutiful to the pentameter as Frost remained, finally broke away from it vehemently and triumphantly in "Purgatory," and he did so with a rapid and common diction that came from the pub and the street, until the lyric and dramatic pitch were one sound, as it is with the Jacobeans. In Frost's poetical theatre, the diction becomes stately, working almost against the accent. It was not a betrayal or a defeat but a matter of temperament. Frost's temperament was too hermetic for the theatre.

:

But something wonderful, revolutionary within the convention, happened to Frost's ear between *A Boy's Will* and *North of Boston*. He wrote American, without vehement challenge. He wrote free or syllabic verse within the deceptive margins of the pentameter. He played tennis, to use his famous description, but you couldn't see the net; his caesuras slid with a wry snarl over the surface, over the apparently conventional scansion.

Something there is that doesn't love a wall . . .

appears, to eye and ear, to be:

Some / thing / there is / that doesn't / love / a wall . . .

That is certainly how it would sound in English, to the Georgian ear. But think American. In that diction, parody is the basis of pronunciation, and there is only one caesura:

Something there is / that doesn't love a wall . . .

That rapid elision or slur of the second half of the line is as monumental a breakthrough for American verse as any experiment by Williams or Cummings. It dislocates the pivot of traditional scansion; and the consequence is seismic but inimitable, because it is first of all Frost's voice, which in metre is first regional, then generic, eventually American. This happened with equal force to Yeats, but with Frost it is more alarming, since Yeats contracted the pentameter to octosyllabics for propulsion's sake, for "that quarrel with others which we call rhetoric," for the purposes of political passion, but Frost achieved this up-heaval within the pentameter. He accomplished it, that is, without making his metre as wry and sarcastic as Williams's, or as pyrotechnic as Cummings's, or as solemn and portentous as Stevens's.

:

Once that confidence sprung to hand and voice, there was no other road for Frost but greatness, a greatness not of ambition but of vocation:

> *Two roads diverged in a yellow wood,*
> *And sorry I could not travel both*
> *And be one traveler . . .*

I am quoting from memory, which is the greatest tribute to poetry, and with some strain I could probably copy from the dictation of memory not only this poem but also several other poems of Frost's. For interior recitation, usually of complete poems, not only of lines or stanzas, Frost and Yeats, for their rhythm and design, are the most memorable poets of the century.

To fight against a predictable tone of incantation was a great task for the American. Yeats could ride the lilt and history of a long tradition. Frost was truly alone, and many of the poems dramatize his own singularity—not the romantic image of the neglected poet in a materialist society but the American romance of the pioneer, the inventor, the tinkerer (if the pentameter wasn't broken, why fix it?), who knows the rational needs of that society, one of which is the practicality of poetry, its workday occupation, the fusion of commerce and art, of carpentry and metrical composition, the "song of the open road." Whitman's vagabondage is romantic, perhaps even irresponsible. Frost stays put, close to stone walls, under apple orchards, mowing grass, his view of the republic a blue haze of hills, rigidly Horatian.

There was never a sound beside the wood but one,
And that was my long scythe whispering to the ground.

In formal verse, tension creates memory, the taut lines between the poles of the margins, and shape is as much a cause of that tension as stanzas and their breathing spaces, also carefully measured between the stanza patterns. Stanzaic structure creates anticipation; and the verbal music, by its chords, its elisions, its caesuras, delights the ear when expectation is confirmed, but with additional surprise. This is the masterly delight of Dickinson, "the slant of light," her assonant obliquities in slant rhymes. But this is a technique which Frost rarely uses. His rhymes are rich and unsurprising; it is their thought, their argument, what he calls "reason," that delights us. The tension that we enjoy in Frost is that of another slant or viewpoint at what was once ordinary, its melodious sarcasm.

Now I am old my teachers are the young.
What can't be molded must be cracked and sprung.
I strain at lessons fit to start a suture.
I go to school to youth to learn the future.

North of Boston consists of monologues and narrative pieces, dialogues in a fixed landscape, with its subterranean terror of madness as in "A Servant to Servants," destitution in "The Death of the Hired Man," black humor in "Blueberries," infant mortality in "Home Burial," and, best of all, "The Fear." But the metronomic rhythm of their dialogue, the inflexible morality, these pinched tragedies in which their narrow lives are seeped, can tire attention. Something mean, sour, and embittered, like the late mulch of November soil, rises from the pages and disturbs us with the kind of punishment that a tireless gossip demands of his hearer. This is a mercilessly moral climate that produces attic idiots and witch-hunters.

It terrifies the outsider in its eccentric smugness; but this may be the legendary severity of the North as surely as a lyric mania and a corrupt languor are the legendary climate of the South. (From Frost to Faulkner.) With *Mountain Interval*, the lyric freshness of the temperature of a brook in spring pours with the usual clarity over its stone nouns. Or, like cows homing at dusk for the barns, they head for the open door of anthologies—"Two Tramps in Mud Time," "An Old Man's Winter Night," "The Oven Bird," "Birches"—slapped on their haunches to ruminate in their fragrant stalls.

Frost is Whitman's heir in the magnification of close domestic objects and creatures, the "noiseless, patient spider" of his writing hand, a Protestant quality, pragmatic and commonplace as a Dutch interior, the "slant of light" that his other progenitrix, Dickinson, contemplated. The same slant that requires the imagination to honor and to record the oblique, as the great Dutch kitchen painters did, came naturally to Frost's sense of composition and balance. The "slant of light" is also a figure of irregular scansion within the frame of the window of the poem, in which the human subject is stilled by the angled light into vacancy and reflection.

Fall approaches, and with the fall, the poetry of Frost, not so much in full flare like the harlequinade of Stevens, but early and late fall, the line or branch of the verse with tentative colors, then the words dropping naturally off the lines into a heap at the base of the poem's column; the mood of "bare ruined choirs," of "My November Guest." That strain of melancholy, so self-posturing in its easy metaphor unless it is dominated by an imagination that defies it, is the interior weather that Frost divined in Edward Thomas, whom he met in England and for whom he became an example and an inspiration. Frost heard the true quiet of sorrow that gleamed under Thomas's prose, a power of meditation that did not use lyricism for spiritual release but for even more unrelenting questions. Frost saw in Thomas another kind of grace, a knightly, doomed demeanor and an alarming simplicity of courage. All his gift needed was a gentle nudging into metre.

Thomas's poems are not minor Frost, and Frost would not have encouraged Thomas to write verse that was only an English rendition of his voice. He could not make an echo of the Englishman because their accents were different, and accent is scansion. Frost was closer to Georgian pastoral than Thomas could ever be to Frost's vernacular. The differences appear superficial, but they are deep. They have their particularities of posture and temperament: Frost belligerently assured, impatient with sadness, Thomas querulous and haunted by an unshakable melancholy; the American full of aphorism and zest, the Englishman carrying a taciturn foreshadowing of his country's pastoral decline, a lament that leads us to Larkin's "And that will be England gone." Tears prickle at the openheartedness of Thomas's bewilderment, his spiritual and syntactical hesitations. We owe to Frost the existence of Edward Thomas's pure poetry. An act of immortal generosity.

We are amazed at the ordinariness, even the banality, of Frost's rhymes ("bird," / "heard"), at the courage, even the gall, of the poet, rubbing such worn-out coins again but somehow polishing them to a surprising sheen. This directness has danger in it, the same danger it had for Wordsworth in Lyrical Ballads; and that sensation of danger is the ground of Frost's technical courage, and our pleasure in its smiling triumph. The slant or half rhymes of great practitioners such as Dickinson or Wilfred Owen are muted pyrotechnics; they startle, and dislocate, anticipation. But Frost's power lies in the ease with which he slides over his endings with the calm, natural authority of a wave or a gust of wind, making his rhymes, with apparent diffidence, a part of the elements, of poetry and of weather.

:

America likes its sages ordinary but reclusive, and without sexual passion or desire of any kind, as much as it likes them—Dickinson, Jeffers, Frost, Hopper—cynical of material progress, and the more cynical the more revered. Frost's image became one of a man whittling near an iron stove in a small country store. He played the cynical American Horace as carefully as any sophisticated celebrity or rough politician, his clauses like curled shavings, dry, crisp, and parenthetical. Sometimes the wisdom can be vexing in its parochialism. Frost was the true opposite of that other sage, Robinson Jeffers. Here, indeed, were two avuncular recluses, outdoor figures, both opposed to Dickinson's confines, or caves, of parlor and chapel, one on the Pacific coast and the other on the Atlantic coast, both proffering rocky, granite-featured profiles to "the elements," one the companion of seals and spray, the other of deer and birds. They are stone heads of reassuring integrity, until we look more closely and see how frightening the cracks are in their classic, petrified composure, how alarming and even treacherous are their ambiguities of crossing shadows.

Jeffers's long line, like a wave gathering and breaking, is already an inevitable self-evident truth, a metre that gathers its reflection to break and shudder the supposed solidity of the shore of the republic, carrying garbage in its wash sometimes, and obviously, admirably striving to achieve distance, not through any subtle domestic irritations but through the sarcasm of rage, from the hawk-height of the sublime coasting on its own serenity. This is almost a barren severity, like the rock coast that his metre celebrates, the diction already Sophoclean without the labor and the complexity, and utterly wanting in the ver-

nacular humor that exists in all great poets, the raw
peculiarity, even provinciality of Dante, Shakespeare, and
the always-colloquial Frost. The diction of Jeffers is the
stillborn sublime, the majestic tone that he considers fit
for a stupendous and humbling coastline. The cracks in
the stone are treated as tragic flaws, not as common mis-
takes.

:

A parody of Frost, on the other hand, would use the doggerel of the greeting card. The trap is the poem, which
snaps back at us and catches our fingers with the slow
revelation of its betraying our sing-along into wisdom.
Frost said it with less venom: "A poem begins in delight
and ends in wisdom." This leaves out the turmoil, contradictions, and anguish of the process, the middle of the
journey.

> *Whose woods these are I think I know.*
> *His house is in the village though;*
> *He will not see me stopping here*
> *To watch his woods fill up with snow.*
>
> *My little horse must think it queer*
> *To stop without a farmhouse near*
> *Between the woods and frozen lake*
> *The darkest evening of the year.*
>
> *He gives his harness bells a shake*
> *To ask if there is some mistake.*
> *The only other sound's the sweep*
> *Of easy wind and downy flake.*
>
> *The woods are lovely, dark and deep,*
> *But I have promises to keep,*
> *And miles to go before I sleep,*
> *And miles to go before I sleep.*

And even this poem, we now know, cannot be trusted. "Whose woods these are I think I know." He does know, so why the hesitancy? Certainly, by the end of the line, he has a pretty good guess. No, the subject is not the ownership of the woods, the legal name of their proprietor, it is the fear of naming the woods, of the anthropomorphic heresy or the hubris of possession by owners and poets.

The next line, generally read as an intoned filler for the rhymes, and also praised for the regionality of that "though" as being very American, is a daring, superfluous, and muted parenthesis. "His house is in the village though." Why not? Why shouldn't he live in the woods? What is he scared of? Of possession, of the darkness of the world in the woods, from his safe world of light and known, named things. He's lucky, the frightened poem says, while I'm out here in the dark evening with the first flakes of snow beginning to blur my vision and causing my horse to shudder, shake its reins, and ask why we have stopped. The poem darkens with terror in every homily.

:

The selection of letters in the Library of America edition is rewarding, but the letters are generally demure, even reticent. There is a crucial letter, however, to Lesley Frost Francis, in 1934, regarding conflicts of technique. This is the letter with the famous dictum about tennis without a net, but it is inevitable that we come across this sort of thing:

I read that negroes were chosen to sing her opera [Gertrude Stein's] because they have less need than white men to know what they are talking about. That is a thing that can be reported without malice.

Encountering this remark in the poet's letter to his daughter, does one sidestep it as a turd in the road, or shrug it off, or condemn its author and his time, but without the shock of insult, for what else is the remark if not American? One doesn't go ravaging the privacy of family correspondence for proof of racism, and in these dangerous times, when any group can scream injury and litigate against the dead, sue History, and demand compensation, the sudden encounter of Frost as a racist should be neither sudden nor shocking but normal for a white New England poet, which is how he suddenly forces the reader of this remark to think of him. But the passage is hardly without a lasting effect. It does something, from now on, or at least for a while, to this reader's delight in Frost, a delight that may now be damaged, owing to the comprehensive honesty of this book. As one stares vacantly away from the open book, one arrives at that moment in the *Inferno* in which the poet concludes: "that day we read no further."

And yet we must read further, especially with American masters. We must read as far as the white whale draws us, beyond the tight, calendar hamlets and harbors of New England and its chapels with their harpoon spires, to a wider and more terrifying space, the elemental ocean, beyond provinciality, history, race, beyond America, beyond the sick anti-Semitic provincialities of Pound or the patriotic regionalism of Frost to a realm that only genius can depict. We must follow Moby Dick, the huge ribbed metaphor of the white whale carrying the freight of the republic's sins as the republic perishes in the whirlpool with a sole survivor, Melville-Ishmael, who is, despite Melville's convictions of racial superiority, a poet. Now that other races and other causes in the babel of the republic have been given permission to speak in the very language that ruled and defined them, must everything be revised by the new order? Does Frost's ironic, jocular accent not apply to them? But it does, because the new order would be repeating the old order if it made a policy of exclusion and an aesthetics of revenge.

:

Pound's poetry does not absolve Pound, any more than a single phrase from a letter by Frost damns Frost forever. One groans or shudders, but one pushes on. Poetry is its own realm and does not pardon. There is nothing to forgive Frost's poetry for. There are, instead, many poems to be grateful for, so many poems, indeed, that the man, the biography, the symbol of Yankee resilience are all negligible, since poetry pronounces benediction not on the poet but on the reader. A great poem is a state of raceless, sexless, timeless grace, and this book, which contains more than just a life, is too full of such benedictions for this reader not to pick it up and continue.

Skimming a great poet's life, we pause when some fact darkens and jolts the rate of the summary, clouding the passage, and we seize on something historical that corroborates a poem. But this is the wrong way to read a poem *and* a life. We know that Frost once walked all night through a swamp and transformed this into those poems of natural terror; and we know he had terrible stomach cramps as a child, that his father was an alcoholic, that "Provide, Provide" ("Too many fall from great and good / For you to doubt the likelihood") must have been owed to the terror of destitution following the cost of burying his father when $8 was all his mother was left with, which was the circumstance that brought them East, from Pacific to Atlantic, to Lawrence, Massachusetts, and made Frost a naturalized Yankee. But there is a difference between a poem and a journal. The poems essentialize the life. The poem does not obey linear time; it is, by its belligerence or its surrender, the enemy of time; and it is, when it is true, time's conqueror, not time's servant.

The much-honored Frost fought his own petrifaction into a monument by dry, didactic humour, but he could not avoid being cherished, and the self-dismissal and wry-ness became a part of the act, even the melancholy. "Play melancholy autumn," his readers demanded, and however chilling the tone, the audiences roared like autumn leaves around the snow-haired figure behind the lectern, and the doctorates were showered on him, and the Pulitzers, and a tribute from the Senate on his seventy-fifth birthday. He wrote in "Birches":

> *I'd like to get away from earth awhile*
> *And then come back to it and begin over.*
> *May no fate willfully misunderstand me*
> *And half grant what I wish and snatch me away*
> *Not to return.*

He himself grew to resemble a bent birch, its flecked bark, its hoarse, whispering words. And he got away. He died, at the age of eighty-eight, in 1963, more of an emblem than any American poet except Whitman, having become decades earlier that pitted, apple-cheeked, snow-crested image that the country idealized in its elders, public and private, bucolic and cosmopolitan, avuncular and responsible. But the companionable and masterful Library of America collection proves that he has also remained. Here is the canonical Frost (which, in its gathering of Frost's lectures, essays, and stories, shows also that he wrote great fictional prose) devotedly and richly presented by Richard Poirier and Mark Richardson in a clear and airy format that lets the print breathe and echoes that easily parodied voice, quirky in its delights but certain of its calling.

> *And then there was a wall of trees with trunks;*
> *After that only the tops of trees, and cliffs*
> *Imperfectly concealed among the leaves.*
> *A dry ravine emerged from under boughs*
> *Into the pasture.*

A widower with a suicidal son who eventually succeeded in killing himself, Frost showed the scars of his devastations in his scansion, but they did not break his metre or pitch it into a rant that broke its disciplined confinement, for the confinement brought the discipline that his sorrow needed, nor did they abrupt it into cryptic, embittered phrases. It is perhaps this steadiness, which lasted a lifetime, that was responsible for his reputation for coldness. It was not that poetry was all that mattered, was all that he had, that made him seem cruel, but that he could close it tight in its frame like a door against foul weather, or light it, like an old lamp, against even worse weather, the black gusts that shook his soul.

(1996)

A Letter to Chamoiseau

I

We know that road around the blue harbour with its immaculate cruise ship, its oil-storage tanks, and the dwindling fishing settlement you describe under an immense, disconsolate banyan, its shacks with their contorted lanes and rusted trees. The road takes us into the infernal congestion of the settlement from which we avert our eyes—Texaco, Conway, La Basse. We know the people who inhabit these settlements, we recognize nicknames given for both ingenuity and affliction. We had our own Iréné, the shark fisherman of your book, our own Ti-Cirique, the ornate *belle-lettriste*, we certainly knew Marie-Sophie Laborieux, the mother of our multilingual fictions, we knew Esternome, her father, and Sonore, Marie-Clémence, and even the bony, delicately elongated Christ, the emissary of Town Planning, the one who was stoned. We know them still by their quarrels and imprecations.

From the dry season, with its baking footpaths that turn into quagmires with the raining months, from scorching corrugated roofs after cardboard, thatch, and packing crates, the place called Texaco follows its own pattern, its three-act rhythm of servitude, defiance, and independence.

And I know you, Chamoiseau. You were one of those urchins with the artificial anger of boys running on a beach, pelting at mangoes and bursting dry almonds with a stone in the treacherous shade of a manchineel. It is this delight which makes the phrases in *Texaco* leap and finish in spray. Walk carefully in the sentences between the windows of the settlement.

Those are your progeny, Chamoiseau, these black children wrestling and splashing salt water into one another's eyes, their wet skin glistening under the blinding aluminium of the gas tanks.

:

Chamoiseau's characters are not only names but beings. Their conduct is drawn from the complexities of sensation rather than of action. We inhabit them naturally, their rages that roar like a rainstorm through a ravine, their sense of insult as sensitive as those weeds that close like shutters.

So, challenged by the formality of a review, I choose a letter, orotund but written in gratitude. The form allows me to be impulsive, elliptical, to indulge in that simultaneity which you call "opacity." Its style, like yours, is adjectival rather than nominal, a style that lies in the gestures of the storyteller, and it is in the metre of Creole. It is what we both grew up with. The countryside at night with kerosene lamps and crickets.

The countryside is the nostalgic, bucolic part. We also grew up with things that are still here. The settlement like the one in your organic, fragrant novel: middens that accrete around our central towns, usually across exhausted rivers, on spits which jut into the ocean, but whose shacks have neat parlours and swept yards under precious breadfruit and knuckled plum, gardens guarded by old tyres and conch shells. This is what you describe with a humming pain, more lovingly than in any other Caribbean novel I have read. It is one whose elation cracked my heart. Oh, Chamoiseau, your filial duty has been more than fulfilled. You have paid our debt for us!

I would press your book into the hands of every West Indian as if it were a lost heirloom, even on those who cannot read. After that formality, I would run through the markets with vendors in the shade of huge umbrellas, past abandoned fountains, stopping traffic with an uplifted hand, entering dark retail stores selling fading ledgers and disintegrating chalks, preaching, "You have to read this book, it is yours! It has come to reclaim you!"

Its prose is like a *mangue,* that reflecting lagoon where mangroves anchor their branches, over which dragonflies skim, kept fresh by a hidden rivulet, and like a midden, it rejects nothing, from rusted chamber pots to water-ruined Bibles.

The anthill of the place called Texaco seethes with the industry of survival, from haphazard foragings of material to build its own paths into an architecture in which a solid foundation, a paved floor, comes last, but despite its damned condition—the condition of Fanon's *Wretched of the Earth*—and for all the passion of his commitment to Creole, Chamoiseau does not look at the settlement with the gaze of a Marxist, as a political example of what racism and exploitation do to a people, nor is the rhythm of the book documentary in its base, like *The Grapes of Wrath.* *Texaco* is a vast epiphany of what he proposed in a *Créolité* manifesto, calling for a new Caribbean literature, but without any polemics, without the third-person distancing of Flaubert. Chamoiseau does not refute his ancestors; they are in the very sound of his French, even in translation. Great ghosts are in his voice, one from another anthill, the Paris that Baudelaire Creolized:

Fourmillante cité, cité pleine de
  rêves,
Où le spectre en plein jour
  raccroche le passant!

11

A civil servant, a town planner, who visits the Texaco settlement is stoned. He represents both the City, the nearby
center of island power, and the Christ of a second coming.
The stone, as if it were thrown into a lagoon, radiates rings
of consternation, of witness and denial. From this, ambiguities begin. Has the town planner become an agent of
capitalism, a saviour-turned-Judas of his own people in the
service of the silver tanks of Texaco, a Judas whose vision
of a New Jerusalem does not include the shacks that have
fastened themselves like crusted scabs on the raw earth?
The settlement shares the name of the tanks that it surrounds like a besieging army, and indeed is their virulent
antithesis.

The silvery tanks are the new Christ's angels and armour, and so Texaco stands on the outskirts of a sort of
terrestrial heaven that offers economic benefits, security,
and progress. But the seraphic, eyeless cylinders are the
dead opposite of the voluble, haphazard wasteland that is
turning itself into its own City, into a planned future
which it once rejected. As the narrator says of the City-
sent Christ, "He was coming there in the name of the city
council to *renovate Texaco.* In his scientific language, that
really meant: to *raze* it."

The stoned Christ lies prone on the ground. The set-
tlers gathered over the body believe him to be dead and
are discussing ways to make the corpse vanish without
evidence when the figure sighs and starts its resurrection.
"Carolina Danta provoked a panic when at that moment
she fled shouting: *'Oy! Dear! His soul's back* . . . (Rock-

bottom luck . . .).' " He is brought to the shack of Marie-Sophie Laborieux, "ancestor and founder of this quarter." It is she who dictates her memories and those of her ancestors, particularly of her father, the ex-slave Esternome. She is an old woman talking to the scribe, a blackbird of the fields, Oiseau de Champs, and of course she is the source, fountainhead, and oracle of all Caribbean legend, a tree in which the writer perches and listens, translating its rustling leaves into his own sharp melody, the twitterings of his beak, his pen. Her gaze is piercing but benign:

Ainsi, moi-même Marie-Sophie Laborieux, malgré l'eau de mes larmes, j'ai toujours vu le monde dessous la bonne lumière.

For that reason, I, Marie-Sophie Laborieux, despite the river my eyes have shed, have always looked at the world in a good light.

"The river my eyes have shed" is an excessive metaphor and mawkish, but the general tone of the translation reflects that of the original.

   :

Marie-Sophie keeps a notebook whose annals become the archive of the writer, a device that the scribe-bird invests with the precise poetry of revelations, the combination of an African sibyl with St.-John Perse.

Au bord des rivières, le sable de volcan est déjà du bon sable. Mais sable du bord de mer est alourdi de sel et travaillé de fer. Alors, je le laissais à l'embellie des pluies jusqu'à la bonne couleur.

By the river, volcanic sand is already good sand. But the seaside sand is heavy with salt and riddled with iron. So I used to leave it to the rain's pleasure until it was the right color.

—Notebook no. 4 of Marie-Sophie Laborieux

Nos compagnons ces hautes trombes en voyage, clepsydres en marche sur la terre . . . et les averses solennelles, d'une substance merveilleuse, tissées de poudres et d'insectes, qui poursuivaient nos peuples dans les sables comme l'impôt de capitation.

Our companions these high water-spouts on the march, clepsydrae travelling over the earth, and the solemn rains, of a marvellous substance, woven of powders and insects, pursuing our folk in the sands like a headtax.

—St.-John Perse, *Anabase* (translated by T. S. Eliot)

In the south, Marie-Sophie, limestone yields me mortar. By the sea, I roast shells and polypary, the Carib way, to make the mama of all cement.

—Notebook no. 4 of Marie-Sophie Laborieux

"The mama of all cement" is exuberantly Creole.

. . . So I haunted the City of your dreams; and I established in the desolate markets the pure commerce of my soul, among you invisible and insistent as a fire of thorns in the gale.

—St.-John Perse, *Anabase* (translated by T. S. Eliot)

There is the same incantatory memory in the litany of Perse's *Eloges* and his *Images à Crusoe*: that of a privileged Antillean childhood on the island of Guadeloupe, for black writers the souvenirs of a *béké*, a person of white ancestry: "In those days . . ." In *Texaco* the mantric phrase *"Noutéka"* meaning *"Nous tait ka"*—"We used to"— pierces with its plangent echo.

Of course "the mama of all cement" is also in Aimé Césaire's watershed poem *Cahier d'un retour au pays natal* (*Notebook of a Return to My Native Land*). *Texaco*, like

Ulysses, is a large prose-poem that devours the structure of narrative fiction by its ruminative monologues, and *Texaco* happily and gratefully acknowledges Césaire's poem as a source. Césaire himself appears in the book, an active persona in public; in private, he is reclusive and inaccessible. Césaire's incantation in his poem invokes an island dawn, *"Au bout du petit matin,"* just as Chamoiseau's *"Nous tait ka"* does. Join the three beginnings "In those days" (Perse in Guadeloupe), "At foreday morning" (Césaire in Martinique), and "We used to" (Chamoiseau), and you have the elegiac Caribbean memory, as calm as smoke rising from blue hills: "In those days, just before sunrise, we used to . . ."

    :

That *"Noutéka,"* that "We used to," of *Texaco* is the real history, the *histoire* seen for itself of a very small territory not seen in proportion to "the great mutations of the world" but one bounded by small, thickly forested hills, or *mornes*, rusted roofs, bright bays, and bleached villages, and far from wars and changing empires.

Every island is circumscribed by that oceanic sadness called History, but the *histoires* recorded in Texaco are not related to the march, the rhythm, of some optimistic chronology which leads from slavery to emancipation to colonialism to independence, or the demand for it; rather, these events are simultaneous, they have only one meaning and one tense: perpetual suffering, habitual agony. The scansion of time is as simple as the monody of waves or the rhythm of two seasons. The squatters live only in one tense, the "is" of the novel's metre. It is this monody that increases the quality of myth in rejecting a linear law and calendar: it is *l'histoire*, not History but the story, the fable, the rumour, as opposed to times, dates, and places. Every event in *Texaco* is given a domestic but mythic resonance, not by the narrator-novelist, the bird-scribe, but by the agitations of rumour, by contradictory memory, and by

the incantations of its characters. One such episode is the
marriage of the roguish character Qualidor to

the widow of a freemason whose body had joined his brothers
on rue Lamartine and whose tomb held only the wood of a banana tree. This was revealed when the tree, fed by no-one-
knows-what, smashed the coffin and shot stems through the
vault, breaking the white tiles and the marble stela, and ventur-
ing three big leaves without ever promising one banana bunch
(good thing, for it frightened everyone to even think about such
inconceivable fruits). Bewildered, the widow didn't go to witness
the phenomenon with her own eyes. Leaving their lodge called
the Beehive at night, the freemasons cut down the banana tree
every month, but it grew back on full moons. That mystery induced a diarrhea of gossip. The widow found herself in a solitude that no fellow dared to violate except for that mongrel
Qualidor. Used to City's garbage, he was able (from what I've
heard, I'm not the one saying this) to approach the woman,
gather nectar from her armpits' sulfurous pollen, undo her grey
laces, roll down her green slip, dust her hair, and live it up with
her, in a fog of incense, dishonorable candlelight humping . . .
Ah, how people like to talk . . .

:

Marie-Sophie's memory goes back to the days of slavery,
when her ancestor Esternome saves the life of his owner,
the *béké*, from an attack by a *nègre marron*, a Maroon, or
fugitive slave, and is given the freedom of being a *nègre
savanne*, a savannah Negro. Esternome falls in with a lech-
erous but indstrious white, fire-haired carpenter called
Théodorus Sweetmeat, from whom he learns the trade,
travelling about the island with a band of freed artisans;
they are attacked by Maroons, and Esternome moves to
Saint-Pierre. He hustles for menial jobs and shares the
pleasures of a woman called Osélia-hot-pepper or Osélia-
tin-o'-syrup with her customers. The volcano overshad-

owing Saint-Pierre will later erupt, but here is life before its extinction from a calendar that is measured by natural disasters.

Békés and france-whites went around in carriages, dined on dinner on the top floors of restaurants, and paraded on the steps of the theatre or the cathedral, whose creamy white stone broke up the shadows. They endured in the districts of Fonds Coré, around the Fort and the Ex Voto parish where all kinds of religious affairs flourished . . . You could see them sipping the falling day under the tamarinds of Bertin Square. One saw them savour the melody of the orchestras around Agnès Fountain. They opened the holes of their noses to medicinal iodines or gazed in open-eyed wonder at the tritons spitting mountain waters.

As it did in Napoleonic Haiti, a civil struggle develops between the mulattoes and the freed slaves, the *affranchis*. The social pyramid, with a black peasantry at its base, a mulatto bourgeoisie in its middle, and whites or *békés* at its peak, is the racial structure of Caribbean history, with the Janus-faced mulattoes seen as either traitors or mimics. Chamoiseau also spurns the *dou-dou-isme* (the sweet-sweetness) of the mulatto women of folksong, common to Haiti and the smaller French islands, with their prototypical *foulard*, *madras*, and gilded earrings. For Chamoiseau, sweetness and slaughter go together in the myth of the mulatto women. But the myth—as sometimes retold from "notebooks" Chamoiseau has invented—has its intricacies of torment, too. In one of her entries, Marie-Sophie reflects on Esternome's habit of labelling each person "according to his degree of whiteness or unfortunate darkness":

Marie-Sophie, don't believe it, sure it was about color but it was also about manners and nice airs. With manners and bearing

they saw you as a mulatto, so that mulattoes were sometimes completely dark. But without the manners or the bearing, a mulatto of skin (same thing or worse goes for the white man) remained who he was. It's complicated but here's the real thread: the best bearing was the skin without slavery's color. And what color was slavery's skin? What color? Not mine in any case . . .
LONG LIVE SWEET-MAMA FRANCE!

—Notebook no. 5 of Marie-Sophie Laborieux, page 7. 1965. Schoelcher Library

Sweetmeat, the flame-haired master-carpenter, expires from syphilis. Osélia leaves the island with a white man, and Esternome drifts in a haze of alcohol but recovers to resume his work as a carpenter and helps build the city of Saint-Pierre. He falls in love for a second time with Ninon, a slave girl whom he identifies with the zeal for liberty. But in 1902 the volcano Morne Pelée erupts, with thirty thousand dead. The capital becomes a scorched ruin.

The pages dealing with the eruption move with the fatal leisure of lava, with the panic of screams and muffled detonations at its margins. There follows a migration to the second city of Fort-de-France, where squatters settle. After Marie-Sophie's mother, Idoménée, and then Esternome die, the oil company acquires the site that will multiply into the shacks of the settlement that takes its brand name, the shacks multiplying through the ages that are called the Age of Crate Wood, the Age of Asbestos, and the Age of Concrete, the age in which Marie-Sophie, the founder of Texaco, dies, in 1989.

III

When I met Chamoiseau, we spoke in Creole. This was something I learned not to do with Césaire, sensing either incomprehension or rejection. My Creole was cautious and awkward, enthusiastic, ungrammatical. There is a difference between St. Lucian and Martiniquan Creole which is more than just in accent but also in tone and even vocabulary. They say tomato, we say tomahto, they say *pain-bois*, we say *bois-pain* for the word "breadfruit," which may mean that St. Lucians speak, by the lights of Martiniquans, poor patois. For us the tone of Martiniquan Creole, like Haitian, is more French than Caribbean, and these points would be irrelevant if it were not for expansive strictures of the manifesto which Chamoiseau coauthored.

This manifesto, *Eloge de la Créolité*, was published by Editions Gallimard in French in 1989, and in a bilingual English/French edition in 1993; it was composed by Jean Bernabé, Patrick Chamoiseau, and Raphaël Confiant, and translated by Mohamed B. Taleb-Khyar. It states: "Caribbean literature does not yet exist. We are still in a state of preliterature." (Oh yeah? My exuberance about *Texaco* should be tempered by this typical Francophony, France's ambiguous bequest, but it is not.) If *Texaco* were merely a philological tract, an experiment that demonstrates the *opacité* of French Creole, my interest in it would flounder by the end of its first paragraph.

Not only for members of the French Academy, but for the last few *békés* and their illegitimate heirs raging on their verandahs, those who were light-skinned enough to have the apoplexy of tangerines, the tract was a part of the tradition it rejected: that of publishing manifestoes. But it also alienated Césaire.

His instinctive fear of illegitimacy often dictated to Césaire the use of the most pure and measured French idiom, enhanced by an impossible Creole, impossible because its literary status demanded yet to be invented . . . As for us, our defense of Creoleness will never be that of an idle and parasitic crouching.

The manifesto seems to be caught in its own trap between the teeth of belief and syntax. What is the plane on which its eloquence, measured and subtle, always on the verge of contradiction, rushes along? The metre of the manifesto's polemical aesthetic is not one of which Creole is incapable, but it is nevertheless academic, even classical, as opposed to the invisible but imagined gestures of the sinuous, incantatory emphasis on *oralité* that characterizes Creole. The manifesto urges *oralité* in the solemn parentheses of the lectern, not of the vegetable market it wants us to understand.

Nothing is more French than the confident rhetoric of this manifesto. It echoes, in its emphatic isolation, all those pamphlets outlining programs for a new painting, a new poetry, that erupt from metropolitan ferment, and that, reaching out to embrace a public, baffle it by their vehemence. What is the tone of the manifesto if not that of its language, French, being used in the metre of exposition? Why was it not written in Creole if it is that passionate about authenticity? In the manifesto we hear really the old yearning for naïveté, for the purified and primal state of the folk of the virginal countryside, with its firefly fables and subdued nobility; in other words, Rousseau and Gauguin from the mouths of their subjects, their voluble natives. This reduction is simplistic, but it probably reflects the antithetical quarrel of English versus French, a quarrel between two colonial conditions, and above all, it is something that *Texaco*, the novel, subverts, contradicts, and then triumphs over. The book is never polemical, yet it was created from polemical argument.

One of the manifesto's grandest aims runs as follows: "*We shall create a literature*, which will obey all the demands of modern writing while taking roots in the traditional configurations of our orality."

:

The torment of the process of translating *Texaco* is for me quadrupled. First the original, the French, then the Creole (one is talking about vocabulary, not tone, which is unified in the novel, hence its miraculousness), then the translation into English, and then into an English version of Creole whose base is French Creole; one must glide, with the translation's push, over some discomforts and perils. Since no two Creoles are identical in the Caribbean—Haitian Creole is different from St. Lucian—the sense of *opacité* increases.

The word *gommier*, for example, translated into "gum tree," is not only the tree itself but also the dugout canoe manufactured by the indigenous Caribs; and as the tree, its sound contains the activity of a light breeze in the gum tree's boughs or branches; "boughs," however, is archaic, containing a mild assonance—*"gommier,"* "boughs"—but it is so right a sound for the Carib canoe in its buoyancy and elegant length, its riding and shearing of water, the carved trunk of the floating tree and the blue echo around the word. But that is in Creole, or what in St. Lucia we also call *patwa* (patois). The *gommier maudit*, "cursed gum tree," enrages because of the ceaseless shedding of its white blossoms, which, once reaped, only repeat their infuriating cascade. Who first cursed them is by now lost, but their Sisyphean rhythm continues every season.

:

Let me reassure readers of the English translation that the prose of *Texaco* is based on a delight in the craft of writing, which supersedes translation, that subdued elation that propels and unites different masters—Joyce, Márquez, Hemingway, Melville—and perhaps that joy's name is poetry. *Texaco* is garrulous because of its *oralité*, because Creole needs that expansive syntax which asks itself rhetorical questions accompanied by gestures, then answers them, a language audibly aware of its melody, its pauses and flourishes, its direction towards laughter even in tragedy.

This continuous bemusement at the ironies and stupidity of fate, of history, of orders laid down by the City (the city as metropolitan law and wisdom) is what gives all the novel's characters a tragicomic grandeur or, rather, an undefined stature that is not modelled on another archipelago's ideas of hubris, on a Medea, or a Clytemnestra, or on the sibylline prophesies of doomed defiance, because Africa's gods have been lost. There is no catharsis, its arc is not Aristotelian, the agonies it describes are not individual but those of the entire race, not unique but those of the whole chorus of the settlement. The tribe discovers its voice in defiance and by survival.

No one thought he'd live: a snake-bite means a funeral. But he, beg your pardon, nevertheless he reappeared in the light of rest-day to visit a star-apple tree that twenty blackbirds were madly shaking.

That "beg your pardon," with an implied gesture anticipating interruption by the reader-listener, uttered with the authority of the storyteller, the *griot*, and of course, the novelist, is the *oralité* celebrated in the manifesto, and for me it is wonderfully accurate in the humour of its inflection, its relentless garrulity, its *"moin,"* its *"tends ça,"* and in English Creole: *"hear dis," "you listenin'?," "I could finish talking?"* This is the echo of the vessel that carries the tribal memory, and not only memory but invention, the magnification of ordinary events, the casualness of catastrophe, and it is at the centre of the novel. The parenthetical phrase provokes laughter, a delightful scepticism, and it attenuates the reader's hearing into a receptacle in which everything is torrentially poured, as such miracles and even agonies did when we were children, a smile that the storyteller-novelist exploits, a confirming nod that foresees a radiant ending, an exaltation, a triumph.

That parenthetical aside of "beg your pardon" is not new, it is part of the convention of storytelling. It is there throughout Dante, as when, listening to a restless and doomed Ulysses describe his death in a whirlpool, the voices of Dante and his character join in an Italian, not a classical Latin, gesture, "as it pleased Another." Chamoiseau does not pepper his text with Creolisms to give it local flavour. It is, organically, the texture, the heat of the meal itself, the crunch of yellow yam, dasheen (taro), white yam, saltfish, and maki (bark beer). I didn't read *Texaco*, I devoured it.

IV

My sensation of Martinique, of the narrowed streets of Fort-de-France, and even the countryside with its goodish roads, was that of an overarticulate congestion, of an extension of the metropole in its subdued longing, with an impatience about its development that made for a melodramatic contrast between modern concrete and atavistic bush. There is a sense of prolonged *discours* (discussion, argument, sophistication) between its metropolitan advertisements and its gingerbread eaves, crowded, urgent, and self-conscious—in short, the direct enemy of the anarchic, quarrelsome, and stubborn anti-citizens of the Texaco settlement.

The direction of the Cité, of the hot agitation of Fort-de-France, felt like the restlessness of the immigrant, not really an immigrant, since theoretically a Frenchman in Martinique is not an immigrant but a citizen. Therefore, as much as Martiniquans are supposed to be Frenchmen, and Fort-de-France is supposed to be France, the Texaco settlement is not French, any more than is *Texaco* the novel. The novel speaks in the voices, the Creole, of its population and not with the centralized authority of the Cité, that is, in the vocabulary of Césaire.

But the novel does not exclude these other Martiniquans, it has rooms and soft chambers, a huge salt fragrant sponge, it absorbs the past, it takes in the civil diction of authority as well as the screams of revolt. The manifesto goes on like a hot road in the noon heat:

This brings us to free Aimé Césaire of the accusation—with Oedipal overtones—of hostility to the Creole language.

:

My hatred of the current way of writing down Creole ("orthography") is a lost battle, but my rage continues in defeat. Coarsely phonetic, it is visually crass, its aural range is limited to a concept of peasant or artisan belligerence that denies its own subtleties of pronunciation, denying its almost completely French roots (if French is allowed to have roots in the ex-colonies, that is, the *départements* of the islands). Written Creole is unreal because the grammar of its African auxiliaries varies from one Francophone territory to another, and in most cases the change proves its autocracy by incomprehensible changes in appearance: *D'lo* for *de l'eau* (water) is only one example. We have to understand that this vehement assertion of creating roots for what, linguistically, is a mother tongue blended with another mother tongue produces a false maternity.

Creole comes from French. Forced or not, Africans spoke French in slavery, and for the Creole Academy this is an unbearable reality. It demands to have its own writing, and its next step, in its effort to go further and further away from the degradation of slavery and colonialism, would be to invent the hieroglyphics of a new alphabet whose echoes cannot be changed unless every surviving aspect of French is banned. The contempt of the Academie Française is ultimately irrelevant.

Written *Kweyol*—why *k* for a hard *c*, for example?—claims an academic and political mandate whose decree I reject because the words arc ugly and their sound cuts off the phonetic subtleties and elegance of the patois spoken in the heights of my own island; and of course it is this idea of elegance which Creole (Kweyol) orthography condemns as being false or self-deluding French.

It is not that Creole lacks elegance. Style is something the French islands pride themselves on, down to their habit of drinking imported wine as well as coconut water and *pomme-cythère* juice, but any language that does more than grunt imposes order, acquires syntax, parentheses, and elegance. The folly, by which I mean madness, is to believe that elegance is treachery, that it deceives the tribe.

:

This is the point at which Césaire stopped, not because he betrayed Martinique to France or Creole to the Académie, but because that is where the passion of argument peters out, in the distant tenor of imposing particulars that are racial despite the protests of a Creole universality. *Texaco* is the combined triumph of the Creole language and of French orthography that Césaire could not visualize. Who is more Irish than Joyce? What is more particularly Irish than *Ulysses*? But where is the Irish spelling of the elegant sentences in English of a true rebel, one who felt himself to be beyond the local quarrel of writing in the Irish language? What *Ulysses* did for Ireland it also did for literature in English, and *Texaco*, also a masterpiece, does the same for another island, Martinique, and for (here one swallows) literature in French.

Joyce was hardly colonized. Chamoiseau's genius, like Joyce's, is too great for any thesis. Of course, this sounds like a trap, this flattery of accommodation, but the waving of banners is a part of French culture; there is a euphony of ideas in the nature of the French language, whereas English, and Creole itself for that matter, have a euphony of images, of simile. This euphony of ideas creates polemic, the polemic of Fanon, of *négritude*, of Césaire and Chamoiseau. The euphony of images is something else.

He brought the oars, the fuel can, and the motor from his lean-to, dumped all of that in a wheelbarrow, and went up the Pénétrante toward his plastic gum-tree canoe, subsidized by our regional council development exports.

Along his way, he saw the Christ . . .

Since Iréné remained somber, however, Joseph thought he was just bringing up one of those black sharks with satanic pupils that no Christian would wish to eat . . .

She was the only one to hear (at certain hours of the day, when the sun smashes the waves with a scintillation of salt) the conches' unsettling song, the hiccup of corals coming up to the surface, the algae's drone, a sort of deserted uproar in the water.

Texaco is not a work clouded by theory. Its edges are clear and natural, and the manifesto may have served as the tillage of its ferment, since the novel's sources are more natural and organic than they are polemical. Its paragraphs rise and descend like the shaggy olive-green hills of the islands; its murmurous narrative is like that of a clear brook through whose corrugated pane you can see the stones. It smells of woodsmoke and the congestion of scorched towns. You can lift your head from a page and see the cobalt sky and enormous clouds of the archipelago. Its details are not those of the narrator but of collective memory: the *histoire* of Martinique from slavery to the revolutions in Texaco's settlement.

v

There is no plot in *Texaco*, there are connecting lives as firmly and intricately woven as a straw basket. Its cast of characters over these hundred years is immense.

Structurally the pages consist of paragraphs that have their origin in that French invention, springing from the alexandrine, the prose poem with its incantatory metre, its protracted breath, the sound of Baudelaire, Rimbaud, Claudel, Perse, Césaire that culminates in the cul-de-sac of Francis Ponge. The sinuous line accommodates Creole rhythms, it keeps its gestures intact. It is not the metre of *"La marquise est sortie à cinq heures"* (The marquise went out at five), which Valéry felt himself incapable of believing. *Texaco's* model is not Flaubert. Its events are in the prosody of memory, of the extended poem-paragraph, and each character joins in the tribal incantation, the chorus, to the one metre, like the chain of a chant, reciting the sorrows of Esternome, his death, the growth of a second city that becomes the capital, Fort-de-France, outside which Texaco sets up up its gimcrack battlements and defies siege.

And what bird should tell this? What warbler of our ragged pastures except the blackbird, who rarely and lightly twitters, with no other plumage but its own sleek African skin, with a beak like your pen, Chamoiseau, swift, accurate without malice? Then, because of standard History, there is this matter of tenses.

Who conjugates the tenses by which these islands are judged? We know those who have made the scansion of the past their own property—schoolmasters, critics, administrators, the French Academy, consuls, prefects, and ironic stylists; those who admire ethnic exuberance, ornithologists who can categorize a Cham-Oiseau, a bird of the Martiniquan savannahs, or *champs*, as a brilliant exotic hybrid.

:

The translation from the French and Creole, by Rose-Myriam Réjouis and Val Vinokurov, often has a stiffened colloquiality that makes the Creole passages a bit arch, reducing its *oralité*, but it moves with the exciting propulsion of the French original, again with an occasional Parnassian flourish that contradicts the sociology. Magic is difficult to translate, and the sibylline can sound ponderous, but the book could not have been so joyous without the obvious delight of the two collaborators and their determination to make *Texaco* a gift.

So across the channel from where I live, a great book has been written; the pale blue silhouette of Martinique is sometimes so clearly edged that one can see the pale hues of houses, or what I think are houses, where you, Chamoiseau, live—a book that for its accuracy of feeling, its intimacy, belongs to the vendors selling T-shirts and their children screaming in the shallows, one that has entered our vegetation, as familiar as the thorny acacias along the beach, one with the cemetery stones bordered with conches, one with the cooing of ground doves in the brown season, and one with the melody of the bird in the dogwood's branches, common to Martinique and St. Lucia, the *champs-oiseau* with its melodic voice and amplitude of heart.

(*1997*)

III / 🌱

Café Martinique:
A Story

I

Across the blue channel from our island, we sometimes saw the haze that was Martinique. Civilization. French wines. Sidewalk cafés for disenchanted love. I went there briefly, and saw what I had imagined, so I have set him there under the blue, white, and red scalloped awning of the Café Martinique; his complexion sallow, nostrils delicate, and the posture erect but ravaged.

Martinique was the Empress Joséphine, a liquid, golden name. Flirtatious folk music, the beguine, madras head ties, green wine bottles with elaborate crests on their labels, and *causer*, the art of gestured conversation. There they drank wine like water. Rosé. Not those viscous punches served in our hotels, in which the waiters planted little paper parasols. The wind off the harbour braced the intellect.

All this was years ago, so there is only a blur of gendarmes in khaki shorts, who wore the hard, round caps known as *képis*; white Frenchmen who carried revolvers. It was the first time I had seen white colonial police. Our own police were local, which meant that they were black and were not armed. Perhaps we had nothing to protect, whereas the sunburnt, thick-thighed gendarmes on duty from the Métropole had the whole of French civilization to guard. Bacardi rum as well as Baudelaire. Bally rum as well as Rimbaud. And because Martinique had such a wide Antillean reputation for her culture, a reputation that reached across the Caribbean like a perfume or a distillery, I thought her gendarmes, as they directed traffic, recited Ronsard to themselves in the heat.

In the glorious days of the café, he had held court right here. All he had had to do, in his black suit, was sit like a spider in this corner and weave his silvery web. His listeners would nod, and the brave ones contradict, as he spoke of a new civilization, of folk music, of how François Villon was at heart a Creole, and how, because it had always thought of time as linear, Europe was exhausted, a civilization that now had nothing left but science. Then his face had the beauty of an axe blade, but he wanted to make it ugly, malign as Voltaire's.

The harbour is a grey-blue, and the hills water his eyes with their iron haze. Yachts rock in the harbour, and the palms rust like anchors. Everything has been the same since that quick glance from God known as history in the tropics. In his pity he smiles the acid smile which has made his face provincially famous.

He no longer reads newspapers. He keeps out of the sun. He does not write anymore, for that is another trap: time as ambition. The face—the flare of the contemptuous nostrils, the thin bridge of the nose, the smudges under the eyes—is like that of Artaud. It has set, in its own mask, an inflexible yet gentle disgust with race. The features, metropolitan though they may look, conceal a turmoil in the mulatto veins as tangled as a rain forest, the blood as brown as the rivers he once praised when he was Lamartine.

To call those jungle streams rivers was the usual betrayal of those who had come here, too lazy or too arrogant to find names for new things. Brief provinces as inflated as their names. A miserable green hillock was a mountain. A rivulet was a river. A district with one road became Alsace or Bretagne, until the alphabet, expiring in exasperation, could only reproduce diminutives. After a while (the stupidity of linear time again!) what was named believed its name, as he had once believed that he was, inevitably, Maurice.

In those days his acidity was as essential to fêtes as lime to a rum punch. His acerbities were preserved and carefully sprinkled on small talk like bitters. His sardonic distance frightened and attracted guests. So one night at one of Madame Beausoleil's high-minded gatherings, a young woman with her black hair sharply sliced across the temples in the fashion of the time had leaned against a white verandah post after dinner. To exhaust everyone, even the stars, to be the last, to talk till dawn almost, was what was expected of him. She stayed through all this, open-eyed till darkness thinned out and trees began to show their leaves on the cool sky. Talk was like ash on his tongue, and outside even the frogs and the crickets had stopped.

There was an edge of morning in the night wind.

"It's such a privilege to have met you," she had kept saying.

But the palms knew nothing about all this in the café where he sat in the shade on this mid-afternoon. He looked at their wilted plumes across the hot rue de Somewhere as, in his mind, he watched himself leave the café. Without stirring he projected every gesture. The body called Maurice left a tip on the table, by a pile of saucers. He had made his own little ziggurat here, because conversations in a Paris café were once measured by the piling of saucers. So Maurice was leaving while he sat still, his projection adhering to a rigid schedule, an inner clock.

He was, after all, a fixture. A riddle that had survived. Pedestrians examined him from afar, like a sphinx. As he sat, his tongue probed a cavity like a snake in a ruin. An adder in Delphi. But it pressed too hard, and a calcified tooth broke off in a fragment of coral, so he curled it on the tip of his tongue and, removing it with a finger, pressed it carefully into the saucer. There, that was history. It was by such little things that we measure entire epochs, not by love. A palm tree blurring without his glasses, a button breaking. They could pierce one more than a book, like the time when, having poured out half his heart in a long, long letter to her right here at this white iron table, the nib broke.

He watched himself walk the street of Negro shacks, punctuated now and then by an aspiring bourgeois villa with its fruit trees, lawn, and chairs in the thick garden. His shadow moved along the walls, and he turned his head.

He thought how he hated those local courtesans who began in their teens the rites of titillation, whose goddess was the Empress Joséphine. He had known too many beauties whose vanity was exactly like the island's. Who wanted poems written to them, who showed, in the flashing thigh of some valley here, the bared knee of a hill, provocations, *oeillades*, flirtations behind bamboo fans, who wanted only to be admired; teasers whose motto was see but don't touch. So he did not try to touch her that summer when she had dropped him off at his rented room on the quiet street.

The next afternoon, after Madame Beausoleil's, she had driven him to a wide, long, empty beach near the volcano, on which the appearance of a single fisherman was as startling as an exclamation point. She had lain on her stomach and squinted at him as she spoke about her own poems and stories. She wanted to write well, she told him, salt glittering in her gaze. She wrote nonsense, silly little stories. It should be her life's work, he said, even if she was beautiful.

Sitting cross-legged on the sand, she had stretched and scooped and piled and patted a mound around her thighs. Frowning, she had scraped his brain empty with the sweet voracity of a child finishing a dessert. Then she would rapidly slap the sand from her palms, her thighs, and her rear and, after making a swift crucifix, dive without a ripple into the water. His heart felt as wide as the bay, but when she came out of the sea, her smile had altered. It was the smile of Eve, he thought, or the mantis, but a smile that changed him from a lover to an uncle. Uncle Maurice.

He watched the paler marks at the edge of her shoulder straps. She was white, a metropolitan, but two years in Martinique had made her skin cinnamon, like a native's. Her face was still a schoolgirl's. He wanted to make it tragic, to put pouches under her eyes, to make her young breasts sag with time, to place the parenthesis of a secret sorrow around a despondent mouth; then she might understand him. Seductions and adulteries had been easy for him. His lechery cried out for an obstruction.

She swam strongly, far, far out, as if she wanted to leave the island. Her hair was a black helmet bobbing. He was worried that the afternoon would bore her. Soon it wore him out, the discipline of keeping his stomach in, of smiling carefully to conceal his teeth, of deflating carefully when she strolled out of range.

I I

During the murderous rain of August, with its plague of rainflies and its threat of mildew, the air in his room was palpable, damp blotting paper. The rainflies fell in his food. His writing paper sagged. The rainflies crawled over it, like an alphabet with its own will. He let her write, imagined her at a windowsill, straining to remember what he had tried to teach her on that afternoon at the beach. The rainflies were the obverse of that tribal parable in which we grow wings and soar towards light. He watched them fall from the bulb and lose their wings and turn into ants. Termites. Frantic as her handwriting. It was the hurricane season, and on bad days the sky was indigo. He would have to turn the bulb on, on the worst days. The awning of the small verandah of the café would be taken down. Then put back up. Then taken down again. This farce depended on the sun. Without the sun all his thesis of helotry and the new Aegean felt soggy, a ball of newspaper in an ochre-flowing drain. It rained and the rain flooded the tiled terrace and the café. He never sat indoors in the café, so he stayed in his room. Where could he sit? There were no passersby to point him out. They would be sheltering under balconies with defeated black faces. He forgot how much it rained in August. The months passed, and he thought of August as dry, rusted, golden, and there would be days when she was, but then the rain would begin and everything would halt in that long, indigo eclipse.

After the convulsions of rainstorms, of tropical depressions, the sun worried its way through thick grey clouds, like a cigarette burn in his blanket. The clouds burned away. The sun came out full. Heat sucked up the puddles in the asphalt. The trees shook themselves like wet dogs. Everything, after involuntary shudders, from chickens to the seminal drops on the electric wires, returned to its normal, sunlit sadness. A season passed, wet then dry.

One day at the café, the waiter brought him a brown package with a Parisian postmark. A magazine and an anthology of short stories. He looked at the contents. It was

a cheap magazine with blurry photographs of the contrib-
utors. Was that her? With even shorter hair? He supposed
so. The hurricane season passed and, with it, the threat
to his mind. And then it was December, then January, and
it was cool and blue and hard with light again, the fronds
of the palms sounding fresh, and when it rained it was
through the sunshine.

He was glad that her small, rust-coloured Peugeot
would not have to pass him on the road and that she would
not have to wave at him and he pretend that he had not
seen. She was beautiful, certainly, but up in the country
there were beautiful women whose skin was the colour of
smoke, of charcoal itself. Their eyes glared, and when they
permitted their high-boned, smouldering faces more than
a taut smile, their teeth flashed white as paper. Knotted
madrases across their brows gave them the blank severity
of ebony masks, the varicoloured plaid of the handker-
chiefs deepened the sheen of black flesh, and these
women were from his grandmother's side. Country
women. The dirtier their condition, the nobler they
looked. Their element was poverty, and when he had
worked for a while at the tourist bureau he had designed
that poverty's emblematic costume. Her clothes grey, dirt-
crusted, soiled, but her bound head in its black profile
uplifted and as noble as Hecuba's. He had fluted her skirts
in the wind to evoke a classical statue, thinking of his
grandmother and his gallery of great-aunts, but of course
they had rejected his design. They wanted reverie, fantasy.
In the end they went back to the usual photographs of
tanned blondes waterskiing, corals under water, immaculate tennis, and a local model in national costume, also
immaculate, parting bougainvillaea branches and holding
a vacant basket, her grin as empty as the sea. He had tried
to market poverty as an idea, as a poetric truth. He had
seen how tourists looked for it on the pretext that they
were seeking something native, real. That was the way he

had tried to pay back grandmere, and to take revenge on his illegitimate white grandfather, a khaki man with a khaki helmet on a khaki horse. He had probably tumbled her in the canes.

The young poets celebrated blackness now, but for him their devotion was another kind of Oedipal rape, or an infantile desire to hide in those skirts, away from the world, away from technology deep in maternal Africa. One had said to him, in this same café, some days ago, "I know why you don't write anymore. Why you haven't written anything for years. It is because of the past. Because of your colour, you cannot face the past. It is shame, that's all."

"Whatever you want." He smiled.

"You sit here and look mysterious while things pass you by. And everybody reveres your silence. But we do not. You do not read us, you don't encourage us. You have no political position. You could help young people. Don't you notice that nobody comes and talks to you anymore?"

"Except you."

"Not anymore."

"I hope so."

"Couillon." He got up to go. He left money on the table. After that, he stayed away from the café for a week. Leaving his emblem there at the empty table. But there was a mould to fill and he came back.

He fell in love again. Implacably, this time. She sat by a window, the light behind her golden, in a white shift. Madame Vigée-Lebrun with her sketchbook. Chiton folds, transparent, fell over her breasts. He could not quite see her face because it was in shadow, like his own in the café. "They do not understand you, my love," she was writing, "but I do."

He did what he had never done in his life before and vandalized a book. He tore the picture out and put it in his wallet. He had found her in the library. Write me a letter, he muttered.

Once more he took pride in his step, the buoyancy of the boulevardier. It is the idea of time, he assured himself, that makes a floating man drown. That punctures him, panics him, and makes him leak like a ribbed canoe. Otherwise, he could last forever, floating on the whim of the currents. It was this resignation that had made him a philosopher, a message in a bottle on the Gulf Stream. He enters his room. Thinking of all this, smiling, he falls asleep.

He sleeps like Chatterton, like a dead matador in *Carmen*. He snores delicately. But there is nobody watching him, except me. Over the trees, down the dry gulch with rocks that have boiled so often in the heat that they have cracked and splintered, and over the nasty brown rivulet where they dump colourful garbage, boys are playing soccer. The thud of the ball goes on all afternoon.

I am writing this letter twenty-five years later. She is taking up her sketchbook and propping it up on her transparent knee, Madame Vigée-Lebrun and her sketchbook, and I write to him, in his sleeping form, because I cannot bear his disenchantments when he is awake. I will not read all of his sad, self-published book that talks about new civilizations. It is too close to my own life. I should compose a plot, cunningly, while he sleeps, and there he would be immortalized.

It would have the hills, first, that he loved young and despised when their proportions became absurd, their names inflated. And small houses on the sides of the hills, and two black women, in clean rags, walking along the side of the road towards the river. The names, too, that he would write and rewrite in his blue-covered then later marbleized exercise books, sounded so rich in themselves that they did not need rhymes. And Renan in the cathedrals by the sea. And Gauguin in the lowered flame of the *immortelle*. And the reefs under the clear green water that looked like bruises, when he was trying to write prose-poetry, and was also a determined adulterer, going through the wives of his friends like doors in a farce. He had his litany of hatreds and they kept him going: the turgid molasses of the harbour at night. Whores suddenly bursting into song before the night began. Country-and-Western music on the jukebox. The lounges of luxury hotels. Women who seemed alone in bars until their husbands came. Berets. Beards. Metropolitan gendarmes. Black policemen. Goodbyes. When she left for Paris he did not see her off. He wanted someone who would never move again. Who did not catch planes whose engines tore up the clouds like paper and broke his heart. Write me a letter, he had asked her. Someone please write to me.

All right, then.

Dear Maurice: There were no sidewalk cafés in my island where we watched yours across the channel, and thought of conversation and white wine. The British don't go in for that. Was Fort-de-France very much like Paris? Was it ever at all like Paris? Did you really see wide marble plazas by a bluish-purple harbour and the philosophers moving around, not in African, but in white robes, with nothing Moroccan about them, though? Did you see the whole archipelago as another Aegean? You never managed to decide what costumes we would wear. Togas. All that wonderful talk! All that invaluable bitterness! Your muse was a black-haired, brown-skinned girl who, mentally, was only visiting. She wanted to be embittered, like you, to know that life was not like daydreams, because she had been punished by having everything: beauty, wit, and laughter that winked off the long-stemmed glasses. And when she lowered her eyelids at some careful crudity you uttered, Maurice, as the poet of this civilization poisoned by Europe—yet blazing-eyed as the plants with your love

a cheap magazine with blurry photographs of the contrib-
utors. Was that her? With even shorter hair? He supposed
so. The hurricane season passed and, with it, the threat
to his mind. And then it was December, then January, and
it was cool and blue and hard with light again, the fronds
of the palms sounding fresh, and when it rained it was
through the sunshine.

He was glad that her small, rust-coloured Peugeot
would not have to pass him on the road and that she would
not have to wave at him and he pretend that he had not
seen. She was beautiful, certainly, but up in the country
there were beautiful women whose skin was the colour of
smoke, of charcoal itself. Their eyes glared, and when they
permitted their high-boned, smouldering faces more than
a taut smile, their teeth flashed white as paper. Knotted
madrases across their brows gave them the blank severity
of ebony masks, the varicoloured plaid of the handker-
chiefs deepened the sheen of black flesh, and these
women were from his grandmother's side. Country
women. The dirtier their condition, the nobler they
looked. Their element was poverty, and when he had
worked for a while at the tourist bureau he had designed
that poverty's emblematic costume. Her clothes grey, dirt-
crusted, soiled, but her bound head in its black profile
uplifted and as noble as Hecuba's. He had fluted her skirts
in the wind to evoke a classical statue, thinking of his
grandmother and his gallery of great-aunts, but of course
they had rejected his design. They wanted reverie, fantasy.
In the end they went back to the usual photographs of
tanned blondes waterskiing, corals under water, immaculate tennis, and a local model in national costume, also
immaculate, parting bougainvillaea branches and holding
a vacant basket, her grin as empty as the sea. He had tried
to market poverty as an idea, as a poetric truth. He had
seen how tourists looked for it on the pretext that they
were seeking something native, real. That was the way he

had tried to pay back grandmere, and to take revenge on his illegitimate white grandfather, a khaki man with a khaki helmet on a khaki horse. He had probably tumbled her in the canes.

The young poets celebrated blackness now, but for him their devotion was another kind of Oedipal rape, or an infantile desire to hide in those skirts, away from the world, away from technology deep in maternal Africa. One had said to him, in this same café, some days ago, "I know why you don't write anymore. Why you haven't written anything for years. It is because of the past. Because of your colour, you cannot face the past. It is shame, that's all."

"Whatever you want." He smiled.

"You sit here and look mysterious while things pass you by. And everybody reveres your silence. But we do not. You do not read us, you don't encourage us. You have no political position. You could help young people. Don't you notice that nobody comes and talks to you anymore?"

"Except you."

"Not anymore."

"I hope so."

"*Couillon.*" He got up to go. He left money on the table. After that, he stayed away from the café for a week. Leaving his emblem there at the empty table. But there was a mould to fill and he came back.

He fell in love again. Implacably, this time. She sat by a window, the light behind her golden, in a white shift. Madame Vigée-Lebrun with her sketchbook. Chiton folds, transparent, fell over her breasts. He could not quite see her face because it was in shadow, like his own in the café. "They do not understand you, my love," she was writing, "but I do."

He did what he had never done in his life before and vandalized a book. He tore the picture out and put it in of our indigo islands—you hoped you had pierced her heart for good. That your bitterness might send her away while your adoration needed her to remain. She chose your bitterness, it fed her gift.

If men cry in their sleep, while they are actually sleeping, I can hear that silent sobbing, and it is, as we kept telling you, Maurice, unnecessary. This is not the nineteenth century. Bitterness has gone, and paradoxes, and the smoke of railway stations in novels of departure, and because of the penitence of fiction, your face in which I might see myself. It's all gone, *flâneur*, boulevardier, the century has turned, and the police are black today. For all your hatred of it, it is you who believe in time, in history. If you will permit me to contradict you. It is you who are waiting. And only you know what for. Meanwhile, the rest of us have things to do. We move ahead.

(1985)